The
fine art
of
confident
conversation

The fine art of confident conversation

HOW TO IMPROVE YOUR COMMUNICATION SKILLS & BUILD STRONGER RELATIONSHIPS

DEBRA FINE

PIATKUS

First published in Great Britain in 2008 by Piatkus Books
First published in the US as *The Fine Art of the Big Talk*, in 2008 by
Hyperion

A CIP catalogue record for this book
is available from the British Library

ISBN 978-0-7499-2863-6

Typeset in Garamond by Phoenix Photosetting, Chatham, Kent
www.phoenixphotosetting.co.uk
Printed and bound in Great Britain by MPG Books Ltd, Bodmin, Cornwall

Piatkus Books
An imprint of
Little, Brown Book Group
100 Victoria Embankment
London EC4Y 0DY

An Hachette Livre UK Company
www.hachettelivre.co.uk

www.piatkus.co.uk

Thanks to fellow members of the National Speakers Association, especially those in the Colorado chapter, who have been genuine in their offers of friendship and support. Gratitude to my loving and patient husband, Steve Tilliss, who somehow manages to restrain himself from inviting me to explain how I can write about skill sets and preach specific communication behaviors that I neglect to consistently put into practice. Lastly huge thanks to my precious offspring: Jared Fine Holst and Sarah Fine Holst who know that mom talks the talk far better than she walks it.

Contents

What's the Big Deal about Confident Conversation?

During the course of your day, you probably had many discussions with people—two, five, ten, fifty. You may have facilitated a meeting, negotiated with your teenager, clashed with a co-worker, moderated a panel, made a sale, or consulted with a doctor ... Perhaps you had an interview, found yourself at odds with a customer, or helped resolve a conflict. Or you may have got the kids off to school, attended a parent/teacher conference, or had lunch with friends.

We might label these discussions 'conversations', but did you really converse? Did you truly engage others in a dialogue? You may have spent much of your day talking, but in the end, what did you really talk about? The truth is that most of us go *weeks* without having meaningful conversations with anyone—co-workers, project team members, customers, and even family and friends.

Lots of conversation is limited to gossip, soap operas, celebrities, popular TV programmes, sports, and fashion. It's probably even fair to say that some of these conversations can be labelled as small talk. Now, I'm not dismissing the importance of small talk. After all, there are times when it is appropriate to engage in nothing but small talk, such as times when you're waiting for a meeting to begin, getting to know a client or department head, or standing in a queue. Small talk serves a critical function—it helps us break the ice with people we don't know and reacquaint ourselves with those we haven't seen in a while. It also helps us establish commonalities with the people we meet, build rapport, and make the connections necessary to build a conversational framework. And, where appropriate, small talk clears the way for more intimate conversation and lays the foundation for strong, enduring relationships. It's oftentimes the crucial starting point (the appetizer) that precedes the bigger, meatier conversations (the main dish) to come.

That's all well and good, but what happens when we—you, me, and the people we interact with each day—get too full from nibbling on the appetizer and don't have room for the main dish?

By now, you've hopefully read my book *The Fine Art of Small Talk*, and you have not only thought about and implemented the skills and techniques I discussed, but have also come to understand the value of developing relationships, building business, and enhancing rapport. So, if small talk is the appetizer, we might label the main meal as confident conversation. Confident conversation is the 'Big Talk' that helps us achieve our conversation goals. When we engage in confident talk, we are trying to inform or teach, share feedback or an opinion, gain feedback, learn something, avoid conflict, ask for something, or motivate or persuade someone to think or do something.

There's something you should know about confident conversation—it's ... well ... important. And it can be pretty tough. Confident conversation usually requires thought, reasoning, respect, and diplomacy. It requires a dialogue, a conversational give and take with one or more people, and it requires good listening skills and patience. With those thoughts in mind, it's clear why many of us stick with the small talk (which can be challenging in its own right) and rarely ever get around to the conversation that requires big-time confidence. Sometimes, we offer uncontroversial opinions on banal subjects because we know those opinions won't be held against us or because we don't want to put in the effort required to engage in deeper conversation. We may be afraid that our confidence will be inappropriate or awkward, or we may worry that we'll be labelled as too serious and no fun to be around.

We sometimes gravitate away from confident conversation to keep ourselves at a safe distance from others and to walk away unburdened by what we might have learned or not learned, by what we might have been taught or not taught. In fact, the four main reasons we don't progress from small talk to confident conversation are that (1) it's an inappropriate time for anything but small talk, (2) we're creatures of (small talk) habit, (3) we risk finding out that we're somewhat mistaken or plain wrong, and (4) we're fearful of revealing too much or of revealing the wrong information at the wrong time in the wrong way.

Conversation—confident talking—is the key to achieving everything that is important to you in your professional and personal life. Confident conversation is the key to your ability to do what you want and be what you want in this world. What might happen if you learned the proper techniques for transitioning from small talk to confident talk? If you could break habits and engage in more meaningful conversations? If you managed difficult discussions and differences of opinion with ease and diplomacy? If you could accept that you may sometimes be wrong, or less unequivocally right than you'd like to be? What might happen if small talk served as a handy springboard for articulate presentation and serious analysis?

In *The Fine Art of Confident Conversation*, we'll discuss these very questions in order to demonstrate clearly the many benefits of confident talk. Because *The Fine Art of Confident Conversation* is a companion piece to *The Fine Art of Small Talk* (they're the two halves of the talk equation), we'll also create a roadmap that will show you how to progress from small talk to the confident talk and how to engage in confident conversation at the appropriate times and in the appropriate situations. These small talk and confident talk skills will help you meet your professional and personal goals and help you create and follow your own roadmap—one of your own design.

PART I

BUILDING CONFIDENT CONVERSATION SKILLS

A ROADMAP TO CONFIDENT CONVERSATION

Learn how to progress from small talk to confident conversation and take your conversations to a deeper level.

Imagine that you walk into a conference room a few minutes before a meeting starts and you see your client sitting at the table. You walk over, smile, shake her hand, and ask her how she is. Rather than small talk with you for a bit, your client launches into an in-depth discussion of some of the technical issues that will be addressed during the meeting.

At some point, you've probably worked with someone—a boss, co-worker, business partner, or client—who skips the small talk and jumps right into the big talk. No questions about how you're doing or how business is faring. No informal chatting about common interests, friends, sports, movies, or family vacations. Think about how those conversations made you feel. Sometimes people forget (or don't know or don't care) that big talk, the use of confident conversation, is usually preceded by small talk. A conversation that goes straight to the big talk can make people feel rushed or stressed. It can convey that the person is rushing to take care of business rather than wanting to build a rapport or finding commonalities from which to strengthen the relationship over the long term.

Confident conversation isn't meant to be a race to the finish. When you're driving, you don't go zero to sixty in five seconds flat. Small talk is kind of like starting your car engine and slowly pulling out of the driveway or parking space. Confident conversation, on the other hand, is more like the process of driving down the road. Relationship building is based on good communication (small talk and big talk), and good communication takes time and effort. You can see why the connection between small talk and confident conversation is critically important. Luckily, the rewards can be both valuable and long lasting.

When you have a conversation with someone, you usually have a specific goal you're hoping to attain. Maybe you're attending a networking event to build contacts, or you may be collecting information to launch your own business, or you may simply wish to discuss a simmering annoyance with your partner. You can't attain your goal, however, unless you know what it is you want to achieve and map out a path that will get you there. When you create a roadmap, you greatly increase your chances of getting where you want to go.

WHAT'S THE PURPOSE OF CONFIDENT CONVERSATION?

Examples are everywhere of unique and different types of conversation. The UK series of *Big Brother* offers a chat room for viewers called 'Big Talk'. There's at least one sports talk show on every radio dial, there's 'loose talk' and 'trash talk', there's 'pillow talk', and now there's 'Google talk'. There's even 'Talk like a Pirate Day' (September 19—mark your calendar!).

You can *talk* someone *around* to your point of view, *talk at* someone whose viewpoint you don't care to hear, *talk back* to someone by responding belligerently, *talk down* to someone by speaking in a condescending manner, *talk out* or *talk over* an issue in great detail, *talk up* something you support, *talk big* by bragging, and *talk sense* by speaking rationally.

With so many different kinds of talk, it's important to clearly differentiate confident conversation from the rest. At its core, confident talk is important talk. Significant, meaningful, confident conversation. Confident talk is the difficult conversation when an anticipated promotion does not pan out or the expected work is less than ideal, or if you have to share bad news like a serious illness or death of a close family member. It's talk that is seen as an in-depth exploration of business, personal values and opinions, political, religious, cultural, or other complex or potentially controversial topics. Talk that provides an opportunity to ask for something, sell something, motivate someone, learn from someone, or teach someone. Business people might see confident talk as the negotiation for a multi-million-pound merger. Parents might see confident conversation as 'the talk' they have with their children about sex. A married couple might see it as discussions about family finances and raising kids.

According to Professor Ron Carter of the University of

Nottingham, 'Big talk' means discussing our ideas and having them challenged so that we may refine them, extend them, or elaborate on our first thoughts. Along those lines, confident conversation might be defined simply as the expression of thoughts or emotions in words, an exchange of ideas or opinions through conversation, a conference or negotiation, a discourse that maintains equilibrium with battling departments or a means of influencing someone or gaining something we want.

Usually, adults don't have difficulty communicating with children when it simply involves giving them directions on how to tie their shoelaces or explaining the dangers of fire, but adults do have trouble communicating when feelings are involved—either the child's or their own.

With these thoughts in mind, *The Fine Art of Confident Conversation* will help you increase your language awareness, adopt the principles of constructive communication, and acquire the conversation skills you need to feel confident and poised in any situation. If you practise the simple techniques revealed here, you'll learn how to do the following:

- Manage conflict by responding, not reacting.

- Formulate messages that are clear and organized.

- Formulate messages that get to the point.

- Direct conversations in order to manage and use time and resources effectively.

- Engage in workplace conversations that invite participation and increase productivity.

- Listen for information and create conversational bridges to better engage others in problem-solving activities.

- Gain the ability to handle difficult conversations.

- Design messages that cover critical information in order to increase influence and build trust.

- Establish rapport and follow through on commitments in order to strengthen relationships.

- Provide feedback and candid communications in a helpful, non-threatening way.

Confident talk involves building blocks of conversation, the kind that can reinforce the foundation of both business and personal relationships. Put simply, confident conversation picks up where the small talk stops.

WHAT CAN YOU GAIN FROM BEING A BETTER 'CONFIDENT CONVERSATIONALIST'?

'No one would talk much in society if they knew how often they misunderstood others.'
~ Johann Wolfgang Von Goethe

The better you work to understand other people's ideas, feelings, and desires, the more clearly others come to understand and appreciate *your* ideas, feelings, and desires. And the easier it is to make sure that everyone is playing on the same team and reaching for the same goals. Working and living with others requires constant confident conversation. On the flip side, the less concern you show for other people's points of view, the less likely it is that they will share your cares and concerns.

When you become a better confident talker, you achieve *more* with *less* anxiety and stress. You gain more respect, influence, peace of mind, and comfort with conflict. You create more satisfying connections with others and build a healthier life for yourself.

- **More respect.** Everyday communication is based largely on imitation (e.g., I raise my voice, you raise your voice; I smile, you smile). This helps everyone feel comfortable. When you adopt a more compassionate and respectful attitude toward your conversation partners, you invite and influence them to adopt the same attitude toward you.

- **More influence.** When you're honest and attentive, you are more likely to engage other people and reach agreements that everyone can live with. You're also more likely to get what you want for reasons you won't later regret. Lies and deception have a habit of catching up with you and can sometimes have dire consequences.

- **More comfort with conflict.** Everyone has different talents, so there is much to be gained when people work together. Living and working with others will always involve some level of conflict, however, because each person also has different needs and viewpoints. When you have a better understanding of what goes on in conversations, you can become a better team problem solver and conflict navigator. Learning to listen to others more deeply can increase your ability to engage in a dialogue of genuine give and take, as well as help you generate solutions that meet more of everyone's needs.

- **More peace of mind.** Every action you take toward others reverberates inside your own mind and body, so adopting a more peaceful and creative attitude in your interaction with others can significantly lower your own stress level. Even in the most difficult situations, you can learn to respond calmly and positively.

- **More satisfying connections with others.** Learning to become a better confident talker will help you explore two big questions: 'What's going on inside me?' and 'What's going on inside you?' Today, people are so bombarded with distractions and 'spin' that many of them don't know their own hearts very well, let alone the hearts of others. Exercises in listening can help you really hear what others have to say and reassure your conversation partners that you seek to understand what they're going through. In addition, exercises in self-expression can help you ask for what you want more clearly and calmly.

- **A healthier life.** In his book *Love and Survival*, Dr Dean Ornish cites numerous studies that show how supportive relationships help people survive life-threatening illnesses. To the degree that you use cooperative communication skills to both give and receive more emotional support, you will greatly enhance your chances of living a longer and healthier life.

THE ART OF CONSTRUCTIVE CONFIDENT CONVERSATION

Constructive talk preserves a positive relationship between communicators, while enabling people to address problems, face challenges, negotiate resolutions, and evaluate outcomes. Poor approaches to communication, on the other hand, can create or exacerbate problems.

Let's say you need to counsel an employee who has a negative attitude, has a personality conflict with a co-worker, or hasn't performed up to expectations. The risk of putting the employee on the defensive is very high, so some managers might take an apathetic approach and avoid confronting the problem altogether. Other managers might take a hardnosed approach that doesn't acknowledge or address the employee's feelings or concerns. A better approach would be to address the issue directly, honestly, and diplomatically using the techniques described below.

- **Problem-oriented talk** focuses on a problem that can be solved rather than on the person responsible for the problem. *Person*-oriented communication, on the other hand, puts the listener on the defensive and focuses attention on blame rather than on ways to avoid or solve future problems. For example, a friend might offer: 'Let me know if I can help you in any way,' rather than making the critique personal by saying: 'You never had a talent for selling.' Stop to think about how your comment might feel if it were said to you, especially by a friend, colleague or supervisor. You don't have to sugar-coat everything you say, but a remark that inadvertently blames someone else will only create unnecessary conflict.

- **Congruent talk** conveys what the speaker is thinking and feeling. While discretion is more appropriate than full disclosure in some situations, we tend to communicate more effectively by being constructively candid, thus enabling listeners to trust what we say. On the flip side, incongruent communication misleads listeners. For example, we might say we don't care about an important topic when we really do, leading to potential problems down the road. For example, my husband's response to 'How do I look, Steve?' is always a 'You look great, Debra!' But how many times have I discovered horrible wrinkles a few minutes later as I check myself out in the full-length mirror and remind myself that I cannot count on a genuine, thoughtful response from my husband when it comes to my appearance? Have you ever had a shopkeeper rave about how great you look in a particular outfit when trying it on in the dressing room, only to discover from a dear friend that the outfit is not the most complimentary when not viewed in the store's funny mirrors and odd lighting? Congruent talk is offering authentic opinions and perspectives so people can trust what we say. Telling a three-year-old child that she has a wonderful voice may not be too much of a stretch but telling a teenager the same when it is not true may set her up for heartbreak.

- **Descriptive talk** expresses objective descriptions of problems rather than evaluations of those problems, while evaluative communication expresses judgement of the listener, putting the listener on the defensive. An example of a blatantly evaluative statement would be, 'Your room is not clean.' It's more descriptive—and therefore more constructive—to say, 'Once you put all your clothes away I will consider your room clean.'

- **Validating talk** helps people feel understood, appreciated, and accepted. In contrast, invalidating communication makes people feel as if they are misunderstood, worthless, or incompetent. Invalidating communication is superiority-oriented, rigid, impervious, or indifferent.

  Let's say a marketing manager reprimands a staff member for releasing a sales collateral package without including a key presentation. Imagine that in self-defence, the staff member says, 'The presentation isn't done, so I thought it would be better to send everything else right away rather than wait for it to be finished. I emailed the sales reps to keep them in the loop.'

  The following responses by the marketing manager are examples of invalidating communication:

  ☐ 'Take my word for it, sending incomplete packages causes more problems than it solves.' (superiority oriented)

☐ 'We never send out incomplete packages.'
   (rigid)

☐ 'Well, I guess you thought wrong.'
   (impervious)

☐ 'Burn new CDs when we get the
   presentation—don't email it out.'
   (indifferent)

Invalidating communication treats the listener like a lesser person, while validating communication shows respect for the listener's thoughts and feelings. Validating communication centres on finding a point of agreement. The marketing manager could have said, 'I agree that getting sales collateral out in a timely fashion is a high priority. However, sending incomplete packages often creates more hassles and confusion than delivery delays. Please call the sales reps to let them know the presentation isn't ready yet.'

• **Specific talk** provides the clarity listeners need. Global statements of problems, on the other hand, often seem too broad and ambiguous; misrepresenting problems and making them seem too large to be resolved. In the preceding example, if the manager told the staff member, 'You confused the sales reps,' the staff member might become defensive and think, 'Only idiots who don't read their email would be confused.' In other words, the manager's comment is too general and sweeping to be completely accurate or to garner a productive response. The manager's comment also doesn't instruct the staff member how to improve. A more specific statement would explain what the manager expects: 'Sending incomplete packages creates more hassles than delivery delays, so let's avoid sending incomplete packages in the future.'

- **Difficult talk** is anything you struggle talking about. Different factors unsettle different people. Someone who conveys their opinion clearly and convincingly may not be as effective at dealing with others' emotions or delivering bad news. A mother with a gift for giving negative feedback to her child without harming that child's self-esteem may have trouble managing personality clashes between the child and her constantly bickering siblings. For example, before stepping in the middle, remember: it takes two to fight. It is important not to place blame, or more blame on one child over the other. 'The two of you stop it,' does not take sides or assume one child is not telling the truth.

- **Conjunctive talk** is communication that flows smoothly from one topic to the next. Constructive communicators use conjunctive talk to explore a topic fully before shifting to another topic, which enables the other party to recognize that his or her input is valued. Disjunctive communicators, on the other hand, tend to talk over other people, cut other people off when they're speaking, and switch topics frequently. A discussion that bounces around from one topic to the next without bringing closure to any of the topics is hardly constructive.

- **Owned talk** occurs when we take responsibility for our statements and acknowledge that we are the source of the ideas conveyed, not someone else. We 'disown' communication when we attribute our comments to third parties. The manager above would have disowned communication by saying, 'The sales reps wanted me to ask you not to send incomplete packages.' We tend to have more respect for people who are accountable for the ideas they communicate and the requests they make.

- **Two-way talk** is a valuable tool at the office, with a doctor, during a teacher conference, and on a dinner date. Effective two-way listening involves actively absorbing the information shared by a speaker, showing that you're listening and interested, and providing feedback, even an action as simple as nodding your head, to the speaker to show that the message was received.

The Fine Art of Confident Conversation is filled with techniques and hints that will help you build the skills you need to engage in important conversations. By the time you finish this book, you'll have the information and resources at your disposal to make you a successful, confident talker—one who knows how to transition from small talk to confident conversation, reinforce the strength of existing personal and professional relationships, and communicate with others in a fulfilling, meaningful way.

It's time to learn more about confident conversation. The open road awaits.

KNOW YOUR AUDIENCE

Actively identify and tailor your communications to your specific audience—friends and family members, your customers, business partners, colleagues, managers, and staff. Consider how others hear what you have to say, and, perhaps more importantly, focus on learning more about your audience.

Whether you're talking with confidence to your brother or best friend, a boss, or a group of employees, you need to tailor your communication to each individual circumstance. Who is in control? This makes a big difference in how you talk and what you say. A customer, teacher, or boss is in control, while a child or employee is not. Putting yourself in the other person's shoes—whether or not you're the one in control—will help you to tailor your communications effectively. In group situations, especially where you're speaking at a meeting or from a podium, ask yourself who these people are and what they need. Then, prepare your presentation based on what you can offer them.

It would make no sense to give a speech about hunting techniques to a group of animal-rights activists or to give a presentation about knitting at a wrestling convention. These are no-brainers, but knowing your audience and tailoring your communications accordingly are usually much more subtle and complex tasks.

What's in a Name?

It's hard to make a good impression or build a long-term relationship when you have to ask someone's name for the second, third, or tenth time. Knowing your audience starts with knowing their name and it is the only way to make relationship-building inroads. Our names are very personal, and people like hearing their names spoken. If you don't know how to pronounce someone's name, ask politely. There's nothing worse than mispronouncing an acquaintance's or neighbour's name over and over.

When you greet new business contacts, customers, and employees by name, you reinforce the idea that you care about them. Similarly, when you address people (whether employees or children) by their name, this will help you set the tone for a serious, meaningful 'confident talk' conversation.

It can be very difficult to know your audience ahead of time. It requires time and thought, trial and error. It requires you to see the situation from someone else's perspective, perhaps even before you've met.

Every audience—every person or group of people—is different. They have different personalities, different expectations, different wants, and different needs. But they all share one thing in common: *they want to be heard.* This is where asking the right questions and listening carefully to the answers comes into play. With that thought in mind, there are some standard guidelines you can follow when talking to different audiences in different situations.

TALKING TO FAMILY AND FRIENDS

Using conversation to understand your partner is a relationship builder. It may seem that you and your partner have exhausted all there is to know about each other. Partners stop investigating one another and many relationships find conversation has become predictable and uninteresting as a result. Take the time to explore each other's personal histories, current experiences, and plans for the future. Probe each other's attitudes and emotional reactions to those facts. Why investigate? Why not just inform? Well, most of us don't just offer personal information about our deepest feelings. Someone must show an interest first. If your inquisitiveness is not genuine, your partner is unlikely to share those deep feelings with you. Your interest about your spouse's thoughts and feelings is essential to her revealing them to you. Discovering his true thoughts and opinions put you in a position to better understand each other.

- What pushes you and your partner to do what you both do?

- What are your incentives, and what do you find challenging?

- What are your beliefs, and how are they put into practice?

- What are your most common positive and negative emotional reactions?

- What are your strengths and weaknesses?

The list goes on and on. There is so much to know about each other, you will never get to know it all. Develop an interest in each other's favourite topics of conversation. Topics drive most conversations. While dating, you both probably tried to discover favourite subjects. You may have had compatible interests when you were first married, but have you kept up with each other's changing interests? Once you may have been able to talk for hours about mutual interests, now you may find yourselves struggling to find anything you have in common. Now is the time to educate yourself about those new interests your partner has developed.

As with romantic relationships, our conversation with family and friends suffers because of the lack of genuine interest. Hurried lives, busy schedules, along with text messaging and email communication, limit in-depth discussion about thoughts and feelings. Face to face or on the phone, 'How are you?' means little more than 'Hello'. Developing a warm, close bond with those we are most familiar with requires inquiry, patience and an investment in truly listening. Take the time to learn about your child by finding out:

- What embarrasses them most

- Their favourite music

- An accomplishment they are most proud of

- Their major complaint about the family

- What really makes them angry

- The biggest disappointment in their life this year

- Their most cherished memory

Take the time to get the real answers from your child. Getting to know your adolescent can be the most challenging. They may cry 'Inquisition!' Not getting answers to these queries? Try putting them to your sleepy child at bedtime. Take them along on a long car ride with limited eye contact! Bring them up at the dinner table.

Instead of simply asking your neighbour 'How's the garden this year?' keep the conversation going by asking: 'How is it coming along this year with so much rain?' or follow up with 'What have you found the most challenging' and 'How did you manage to make it a success?' When asking about a friend's bike holiday be sure to indicate your sincere interest by asking follow-up questions such as: 'What did you enjoy the most?' or 'Describe a typical day.' You are bound to enjoy deepening, more confident conversations once you make the effort to dig in deeper, listening carefully for cues that will help you build the relationship. Listening carefully brings rewards. You may learn that your friend visited his home town while on the bike holiday. Then explore that titbit of information or save it for another time in order to increase your knowledge of your friend and his activities.

TALKING TO A CO-WORKER OR COLLEAGUE

Good communication in the workplace involves a collaborative dialogue. Even at the office, it takes two to tango, meaning that you and your colleague are both responsible for the communication that transpires between you. In other words, if there's a miscommunication, you're both at fault. The goal is to focus on how you can use communication to resolve the problem rather than aggravate it by pointing fingers.

If you need to discuss a problem with a colleague, ask to speak to him or her when you're both calm. When you talk over the problem, choose your words carefully to make sure you convey information clearly and eliminate extraneous details. This is a situation where some of the types of talk I discussed in Chapter 1 become very important. Problem-oriented talk, descriptive talk, validating talk, specific talk, and two-way talk will go a long way in workplace communications. Vague, rigid, or blaming talk will have a potentially disastrous effect.

Say what you need to say—nothing more, nothing less. Don't make accusations. Acknowledge that you disagree while also reinforcing points of agreement. Eliminating emotionally charged statements and working from a foundation of shared agreement will make it easier for you to ask for—and get—what you want.

Perhaps most importantly, keep your conversations private, respectful, and drama free. Remember, you have to work with this person every day, and, chances are, your colleague won't forget your public antagonism or criticism tomorrow, next week, or even next month. Pay attention to your colleague to learn his or her hot buttons, and steer clear of them. Most importantly, don't aggravate the situation by gossiping about it. Keep the outside parties where they belong—outside. If you need to blow off steam about it, confide in someone outside the company, not another colleague. Focus on what you want to accomplish (your short- and long-term goals), and structure your confident conversation accordingly.

TALKING TO CUSTOMERS

Generally speaking, you talk to customers to build rapport, reinforce your relationship, or sell something. Because customer communications are goal oriented, the better you know your customers, the better your chance of achieving your goal.

The best way to earn your customers' goodwill is to present yourself as humble, respectful, and politely inquisitive. You know more about your business than your customers do, so make them comfortable by explaining information from their point of view. Watch for clues that the customer is becoming confused, and ask if there is a need for clarification. When talking to non-technical customers about technical details, focus on people and actions rather than on code, jargon, and systems.

What do your customers need to know, and what's the most effective way to make sure they know and understand it? Ask good questions. Determine the right questions to ask by doing research. Learn about your customers and their businesses, and draw upon this information when discussing your products or services. Provide specific information that tells your customers what's in it for them and why they should care. Will your product increase efficiency and staff productivity? Are your company's services more reliable and more cost-effective than those of your competitors? The more you know about a customer's specific needs, the more you will be able to target your sales approach.

Targeted Selling

Think of the last time a door-to-door salesperson tried to sell you something you'd never buy in a million years. Or when a car dealer tried to get you to pay for features you didn't need. Don't waste your time or your customers' time with generic sales pitches. Build a loyal customer base by showing that you understand what your customers want and need.

The key is customer service. That means telling customers what they want to hear without lying or bending the truth. Try the following:

- Ask open-ended questions like 'How can I help?' to begin the conversation in a positive way and give your customers a chance to give you clues about how you can target your approach.

- Customers seek products and services to solve a problem, so if you can fix it, you're likely to keep their business.

- Demonstrate your ongoing commitment to your customers by keeping them posted on future developments. Let them know when a new product might be of service to them.

- To build a trusting, thoughtful relationship, ask if your customers have any questions.

Prevent tension with customers. Instead of: 'The damage won't be fixed for a week,' offer: 'The item will be repaired next week.' Instead of: 'There will be a delay in your order,' say: 'We will ship your order as soon as possible.' When a customer complains and you respond with: 'This delay is completely unacceptable. Of course you must be angry,' it is more difficult for him to say 'This is unacceptable. I'm angry.'

Learn all you can about your customer's business, and you'll create the best possible odds of selling your product or service to that customer.

TALKING TO BUSINESS ASSOCIATES

A negotiation with business associates—whether within your own company or from another company—certainly qualifies as confident talk. Just as you research your customers, you need to know as much about the characters involved in a negotiation as you can. With that in mind, think in terms of two kinds of data that you must gather: *task-related information* and *background information*.

Task-related information is collected for a specific purpose and related only to the matter at hand. If you're working on a business plan, for example, you may need to know projected labour market trends for people with a key skill.

If time is of the essence and little is at stake, task-related information may be sufficient. Usually, however, you also need background information in order to understand the personalities involved, the environment in which they work, and the way they have done business in the past. Without this information at your disposal, someone might bring up an unknown fact that knocks down your arguments and causes the negotiation to unravel.

Evaluate the deal and determine how much time you need to spend on your research. If the consequences are great, you will need as much information as possible. There are a number of things you can do to build your background information:

- Read a newspaper or news website which is respected for its journalism, such as *The Economist.*

- Read magazines dedicated to the industry in question to learn as much as you can about the way the business is run.

- Interview experts in the field.

- Study the customers that the company serves and look for the similarities between them.

- Research the company's goals and objectives.

- Read articles or corporate newsletters regarding the company to determine what problems it faces.

- If you really need to know something that you cannot find through research—*ask.*

The Problem with Assumptions

Vague terms mean different things to different people. When your partner promises to help more around the house do not guess that the two of you share the same definition for 'helping around the house'. Ask her to describe what she hopes you will contribute in the way of housework. If you tell a colleague you'll finish a report 'soon', he may expect it on his desk by the end of the day, when your idea of 'soon' meant the end of the *week*. Clarify the details in order to manage expectations.

TALKING TO A BOSS

Talking to your boss about important workplace matters can be a recipe for an emotional confrontation. As difficult as it may be, it's in your best interest to keep your emotions in check, or you may wind up hurting your cause. Raising your voice or crossing your arms can be taken as signs of aggression, so take a few deep breaths before you walk through the door.

Informing your boss that you'd like to discuss an issue is much less confrontational than saying you have a huge problem with her management style. Even if you have a legitimate complaint, direct criticism of your boss may seem like a challenge to her authority, especially if you criticize her in front of co-workers or customers.

Always keep important conversations with your boss

private, discuss issues in general terms, and note the responsibility everyone has played in the situation rather than blaming your boss or others. Keep a positive attitude, and act like a team player, even if you're not feeling like one at the moment.

Approach situations from a solutions-oriented perspective rather than a problem-oriented perspective. For example, you might say, 'The telephone procedure doesn't seem to be working as well as it could, and I had some ideas about how we might improve efficiency there. Could we set up a time to discuss this?'

If criticism is directed at you, try not to immediately become defensive, as this will just cause a communication breakdown. Take a deep breath, and stay quiet, continuing to listen. When your boss has finished, briefly own up to any responsibility you have in the situation, and begin to think about solutions. You might say, 'Yes, my thinking was to prevent clients from getting the wrong idea, but I can see how my approach hasn't worked as I had hoped.' If you have ideas about how to solve the problem, offer them to your boss. If you are at a loss as to how to improve the situation, ask your boss to help you formulate solutions that will be to everyone's advantage. You could say, 'I really do want to improve this procedure, but I'm uncertain as to best way to handle it. Can we work together to come up with viable solutions?' Show that you are willing to cooperate until you reach the best possible outcome.

Don't make guarantees you can't deliver, however, in an effort to impress your boss. This approach will backfire in the end. Be realistic when you tell your boss what you'll do, and make sure you do what you promise.

What to Say to a Thumbs Down

It's not easy to challenge a decision from the boss, especially one as disappointing as being passed over for promotion or a raise. Take the time you need to compose yourself, and then set up a meeting with your supervisor to discuss why you didn't get the promotion and to let him know that you really wanted the promotion. Determine the issues or skill sets that you need to work on to improve your chances of landing that job in the future. Consider asking your boss to become your mentor.

Make the effort to listen for information and input in the form of criticism that will help you to advance. Tell yourself, 'As hard as this is, this is something I need to hear.'

Set aside undeserved criticism with the simple statement, 'I'm sorry you see it like that,' or 'I'm sorry you feel that way.' Accusations such as 'You have never supported me and it shows,' or 'You constantly criticize my work,' draw defensive responses. As an alternative, try 'I do not feel that my contributions are recognized.' Prepare to be your best advocate. For example: 'From what you've told me, I can appreciate how you came to the conclusion that I'm not a team player. I think I am. When I point out concerns with a project, I'm looking at its long-term success. I don't mean to be negative, although I may be seen that way. Can we talk about how these concerns can be communicated so that my intentions are not misunderstood?'

What to Say to a Thumbs Down

Remember: 'Courage is resistance to fear, mastery of fear, not absence of fear'—Mark Twain

---

TALKING TO EMPLOYEES

Employees will be very sensitive to any condescending attitudes on the part of managers and supervisors. So, be extra careful never to talk down to an employee, which is a surefire recipe for conflict and ill will. If you practise *specific talk* with your employees, communicating your standards and values, they will be able to make better decisions and avoid mistakes. Keep them in the loop on office news and decisions that affect them. And while it's easier to send an email than to chat with an employee face to face, certain conversations need to take place in person. Make yourself available. Allow time for individual meetings and conversations to demonstrate your genuine concern for your employees.

One of the most important things a manager can do is to give employees detailed feedback. You can't expect positive behaviour to continue or negative behaviour to cease unless you communicate your expectations. *Tell your employees exactly what you want them to do, as well as when and how you want them to do it. Then listen to what they have to say in response.* Employees are more inclined to work through issues collaboratively when their managers make time to listen.

Begin and end tough conversations with a positive statement, using the pronoun 'we' instead of 'you'. This will prevent your communication from sounding accusatory, and it will reinforce your respect for the employee. Practising *validating talk* when communicating with employees will lessen the inevitable vulnerability they feel in the presence of a manager or supervisor. For example, you might say, 'I appreciate the efforts you've made in compiling these complex mailing lists. I know it hasn't been an easy task, but I believe we need to rethink how we're keeping track of the lists. Could you now keep a running tally of the numbers within each list and report to me each week?' Compare this approach to confident talk with, 'You're not keeping track of the lists properly. Keep a running tally of the numbers from now on.' How would you feel if someone said this to you? Not only has the employee been told he has done something wrong, but he hasn't been told how frequently he should keep the tally or where he should deliver the numbers.

Delivering a less than stellar performance review is not always easy. State the facts, 'Your production is down and there is a problem with …' along with a message of empathy for her reaction: 'This is probably not what you wanted to hear but this needs to be improved, and it starts with ….' Be direct, but don't be offensive. Just because Donald Trump declares 'You're fired!' on the US version of *The Apprentice* every week, it does not mean that is in any way a tactful way to relieve someone of their job. Even Donald admits that in real situations he is more likely to say 'Hey, it isn't working out.'

The only way to be a talented confident talker when communicating with employees is to put yourself in their vulnerable shoes and speak as you would like to be spoken to.

TACKLING DIFFICULT TALKS WITH CONFIDENCE

Give thought to the desired outcome or goal of your discussion before blindly jumping into that discussion. You may believe you have worthy goals, such as enlightening a fellow board member or enhancing the connection with your university-bound child, only to become aware that your language is judgemental or somewhat patronizing. You want to be encouraging, but you end up reprimanding. Some goals are more useful than others. Work on yourself so that you enter the conversation with a supportive objective. Evaluate the assumptions you are making about the other person's intent. You may feel slighted, demoralized, ignored, or disrespected, although that may not be their intent.

How is your mind-set toward the difficult conversation influencing your perception of it? If you think the discussion is going to be unbearably difficult, it probably will be. If you believe that whatever the outcome, something positive will come of it, that will probably be the case. Examine your assumptions and modify your attitude for maximum effectiveness.

Consider your opponent. How are they viewing this situation? How do you think they perceive the problem? What are their worries, doubts, and fears? What would their solution to the problem be? This is the beginning to reframing your opponent as a partner.

The following are suggestions for introducing difficult discussions:

- 'I would like to talk with you about our constant bickering in the hope that we can get along better.'

- 'I'd like to discuss _____ with you, but first I'd like to hear your thoughts.'

- 'I'd like to come to an agreement about _____. I really want to hear your feelings about this and share my perspective as well.'

- 'There is something I'd like to talk with you about that I expect will improve our work together.'

- 'Do you have some time to talk? I need your help with what just transpired.'

- 'I'd like to discuss the _____. We may have different ideas on how best to _____.'

As you gain confident conversation skills think about how others regard what you have to say and pay attention to the nuances of your audience.

3

Manage the Conversation

Discover how to keep the conversation on track and stick to an agenda.

How many exchanges have you experienced that went nowhere? Has setting limits for computer time with your twelve-year-old daughter deteriorated into a screaming match? Do you ever wonder what you were initially angry about when arguing with your partner? Without an agenda or purposeful direction the conversation can go off on one tangent after another. Before you know it, the conversation is over and little or nothing has been accomplished. Face-to-face meetings can achieve much more than telephone chats, text messaging and emails, but without a clear purpose, getting together for a purpose beyond just chit chat is simply a waste of time and maybe even money. An interaction with the doctor over a much-anticipated examination may not provide all the answers to your questions unless preparation has been made beforehand. Meeting with your child's teacher for an update on their progress is not satisfying unless you leave with your questions answered.

Keeping a conversation, on track, however, can be a fine line between sticking to your schedule and your own personal agenda and allowing for differing points of view, possible emotional responses, and additional unexpected information to come forward. So how can you maintain a balanced approach and accomplish your objectives?

FRIENDS AND FAMILY

Exchanges in our personal life require just as much thought and attention as those in the workplace, although rarely do we invest the same thought and consideration as we do for our 'professional' conversations. Frequently we allow ourselves to answer a phone, throw up our hands in despair, march out of a room in disgust, or simply neglect to solicit another point of view just because we are not in the workplace but instead at home or in some other familiar setting. Serious dialogues related to significant emotions and events are meant to be opportunities for learning, garnering resources, determining resolutions or expectations, and expressing feelings. This will not happen without discipline and preparation, whether at home or at work.

The most important element for a successful discussion is to focus on desired results and to keep them in mind. Suppose your child asks you a tough question (about sex, death, etc.), find out what she already knows by asking 'What have you heard?' or 'Why do you ask?' Your child will tell you what she understands—or misunderstands—and ideally what concerns are prompting her question. A child who asks 'What is a suicide bomber?' may simply be asking if she is safe, rather than asking for a detailed definition. Reassure her about her safety. Keep your answers simple. Give answers that are appropriate for your child's age. Describe some of the reasons she is safe by saying, 'Policeman are there to protect us,' or, 'This special booklet describes how to stay safe on the aeroplane.' Ask more questions. 'I feel sad those people got hurt. How do you feel?'

We cannot hope to resolve disputes, clarify expectations, and allow all points of view to be heard during a family meeting or a disagreement with our partner without agreeing to an allotted time without distractions or interruptions. Before you begin a difficult conversation with a friend or family member, know what the issue is and what you'd like to see as a solution. Not determining both the issue and desired result is a big obstacle to communication. Many times, we find ourselves 'making our point' for five minutes or so, finally stopping and realizing that we have no idea what we were expressing. The bewildered look on a husband's, mother's, child's or friend's face tells us they are even more at a loss. Know what your point is and what you need before you start talking. Then stick with that without including other issues or infractions existing from day one. My partner and I joke about my 'Pearl Harbor' file, the database I have stored over the years containing every infraction and slight I see myself enduring, then pull out of the file during a heated exchange, although not connected even remotely to the discussion at hand! Preparing with an agenda of what your point is and what you hope to gain will help create an understanding between you and your partner in the moment. If you think of something you know should be addressed, write it down if you are concerned you might forget. If there is something very serious to discuss, make a special time for just that subject. Don't hesitate to tell your partner, 'We need to talk about _____, when we can get together?' Get started by disclosing the issue you want to discuss in a couple of sentences, giving a specific example that illustrates the issue, situation or behaviour you want to change. For example: 'I am disappointed to learn that you have been gossiping about my divorce. It really hurts my feelings.' State how this impacts you, your friendship and how you fear others in the community might view you: 'It is really embarrassing to learn that people now know about my partner's gambling problem.' Offer how you may have contributed: 'I know I have been a gossip about others in the past so I imagine you thought I would not mind the same in return. I should have asked that you keep my business and our private talks to yourself.' And then state your wish to keep the friendship and let bygones be bygones: 'Our friendship is dear to me. I wanted to be sure to discuss this with you so it did not happen again and I could feel open about sharing my life with you.'

MANAGE A NEGOTIATION BY SETTING AN AGENDA

'Agendas' can be adapted for personal use, as well as for businesses. Open the negotiations by outlining your requirements or terms and conditions, and try to get those on the other side of the table to reveal their starting point for negotiations.

With a spouse: 'I need to find a way to build some free time into my weekends so that I can count on getting a workout in either Saturday or Sunday.'

With your child: 'Your new job seems to be impacting your schoolwork. We need to find a balance that works for you and is acceptable to us.'

With a budding romantic partner: 'Our time together at weekends is something I look forward to but find difficult to juggle when plans are made with such late notice. Can we plan a bit earlier in the week so I can have more time to get my life organized?'

With a friend: 'What can we do about staying in touch now that I am moving overseas?'

Relationships are sure to benefit when resentments and misunderstandings are revealed and eliminated because we solicit this type of dialogue. Focus on the best way to achieve your goals.

Consider preparing talking points or a simple outline in

your mind before heading into conversations that may be potentially explosive with a partner or friend, or an extremely important conversation with a doctor or teacher. Some examples of dos and don'ts:

To a child's teacher do not say: 'Amy always gets As. There must be a mistake.'

Instead say: 'Can we talk about Amy's grade? This is out of the ordinary for her.'

To a partner do not say: 'You should have let me know when the balance on the account dipped so low so I could deposit additional funds.'

Instead say: 'In the future, if the bank account dips below 50 could you let me know so I can deposit more cash?'

Since we cannot undo the past we can direct conversations to produce positive outcomes. As the saying goes: 'We can't motivate people to do better by making them feel bad.'

Visiting a doctor's office can make you nervous, impatient, or even scared, therefore a critical opportunity to manage the conversation. You may have only a few minutes with your health care provider. Later, you might remember something you forgot to ask. Or you may forget what the doctor or nurse said. Being prepared, and creating some kind of 'agenda', can help you get the information you need. Since you are an expert on the important things about your symptoms and your health history, review them before entering the examining room. Tell your doctor what you think he or she needs to know and be ready to ask questions. If you don't, your doctor may think you understand everything that was said. Be prepared by writing down your questions before your visit. List the most important items first to make sure they get asked and answered.

Tips for Managing Conversations with Friends and Family

- Know what your purpose is and stick with it.

- Do not take verbal attacks personally.

- Don't assume they can see things from your point of view.

- Consider role playing the conversation with a friend before holding the real one.

- Mentally practise the conversation. Contemplate possibilities and visualize yourself handling them easily.

- Avoid trying to control the other person's reaction.

BUSINESS MEETINGS

To keep business meetings moving along, write the goal next to each item on the agenda, and note if a decision is required. This will help your attendees to stay focused on the tasks at hand. Otherwise, people can bring up unrelated issues, and the meeting may veer off and never return to the important matters at hand. Circulate your agenda prior to the meeting to alert everyone to the subjects to be discussed, and ask if anyone wants to add a topic. This should prevent most people from bringing up a non-agenda item during the meeting.

Agenda items may have overlapping elements, however, that cause someone to bring up a subject that appears later on your list. If this happens, you can say, 'Yes, thank you for bringing that up, but can you hold your thought for the time being? We will get to that area when we reach item #7.'

Estimate how long it will take to discuss each subject, and then add extra minutes for unexpected, but necessary, discussion. Add up the time for each item on the agenda to determine how long the meeting must be. You don't have to share your time schedule with your attendees, but note this information on your own copy so that you can keep the meeting focused. If others are expected to make presentations at the meeting, however, let them know in advance how much time they will be allotted.

Take a Break

Decide where the breaks should occur, and insert them into your agenda. Most people can concentrate for no more than 45 minutes at a time, so schedule short breaks (perhaps five minutes) as frequently as necessary to keep everyone engaged. If the meeting will be long, schedule one or two longer breaks for refreshments and toilet visits. Don't forget when tackling tough topics with friends and family to be just as sensitive to their comfort and how much time they have available.

While you want to put the most important items at the top of your agenda, be careful not to put two long and difficult issues back to back. Drop a shorter and easier item in between to give everyone a break. Items that are less important should fall to the bottom of the agenda, but if these matters are consistently left behind, you may have to make them a priority at a subsequent meeting.

Avoid serving food at mid-day meetings, as people will become drowsy after eating. Bear in mind that everyone will expect you to keep the meeting focused. It is your responsibility to make the meeting a fruitful experience for everyone involved. This may entail your being direct with a comment such as, 'We're getting off topic, and we need to return to the agenda in order to reach our objectives. We need to table this discussion, but we can always add it to a future meeting agenda.'

- **Before the meeting**, double-check to make sure everything you need is in place. Nothing will stop the concentration like an interruption at an inopportune moment to find a missing piece of equipment. If you must stop in the middle of a discussion for a phone call or other problem, return as quickly as possible.

- **When the meeting begins**, divert from your time schedule only if the discussion is very productive and is accomplishing your goals. When the conversation goes off on a tangent, gently remind everyone of the matter at hand, especially if a decision needs to be made. If someone brings up a topic that is not on the schedule, suggest that it be discussed at a subsequent meeting. You might also ask this person to do some work on the issue and create a report, or you might form a committee to investigate the subject for future discussion.

- **After the meeting**, be sure to follow up by sending the minutes to all attendees. If specific tasks have been assigned, make sure everyone receives these in writing.

HANDLING HECKLERS DURING
PRESENTATIONS

Michael Richards (who gained huge fame in the USA as Jerry Seinfeld's sidekick on the long-running and hugely popular TV sitcom *Seinfeld*) has given us a lesson in what *not* to do with a heckler in the audience. His comedy club tirade began after two clubgoers shouted at him that he wasn't funny. He called the two black hecklers the 'n-word' and enthusiastically referenced a time when black people were often victims of civil rights abuses. He then paced across the stage taunting the men for interrupting his show, peppering his speech with racist slurs and profanities. Clearly, Michael Richards went into a rage in response to 'hecklers' in his audience, a rage that has no reasonable explanation. However, what *do* you do if someone pulls your speech off course? Whether you are required by your profession to be good on your feet or find yourself offering the pros and cons for an extension for your church, managing a presentation so that it stays on track is the key to getting your message across.

The most common problem when you're giving a presentation is a string of questions from the audience. The best way to handle this is to inform everyone in advance that questions will be taken at the end of your speech. This allows you to make sure the audience follows the flow of your information, and it prevents you from wasting time on questions that might be answered later in your prepared material. If someone blurts out a question or raises their hand before the end, politely remind them that it will be of benefit to everyone to wait until you've finished to ask their questions.

Of course, even if you take questions at the end of your presentation, someone may continuously ask irrelevant ones. When this happens, politely ask the questioner to explain how their subject relates to your topic. If the question is still irrelevant, answer with one sentence. If the questioner refuses to stop asking off-topic questions, offer to meet with this person briefly after the presentation in order to continue for the benefit of the rest of your attendees. If you allow someone to control you in this way, you will not only cheat the rest of your audience, but you will come across as weak.

Sometimes, two people in the audience insist on having a conversation during your speech. The best way to deal with a distraction like this is to continue your presentation as you walk toward the area where they're sitting and look in their direction as you speak. You needn't stare at them, but eventually, the entire audience will look their way, and the conversation will stop. You can do this in a subtle manner that sends a clear but gentle message.

Do just the opposite; however, if a mobile phone begins to ring during your speech. Walk in the direction *away* from the sound to keep the audience's focus on *you*, not the phone. If you have an opportunity to point to an illustration behind you or show a slide at that moment, do so. This will ensure that everyone's eyes and ears stay with you. Or employ humour: 'Would it be all right if we all said "hello" as well?' you might ask from the podium!

When Someone Becomes Hostile

If an attendee becomes hostile, it is best to acknowledge the comment and say, 'Everyone has a right to their opinion. I respect yours even if I don't agree. Thanks for offering a dissenting viewpoint, but I want to make sure everyone has a chance to ask a question.' If the attendee continues to be hostile, you may have to ask for his or her removal, but try to defuse the situation before you resort to ousting someone from the room. Humour is very helpful if you can muster it in the moment. If not, be firm but polite. You might say something like, 'I'm sorry that you dislike the topic being discussed, but this is the agenda that we have set for today.'

KEEPING JOB INTERVIEWS FOCUSED

Whether you're the interviewer or the interviewee, you have a responsibility to keep an interview on topic. If you're the interviewer, you need to make sure you ask all of the necessary questions to get a good sense of the prospect's personality, background, and skills. Prepare your questions ahead of time, based on each individual. Asking nothing but generic questions will not only be boring for the interviewee, but such questions are less likely to give you the information you need. A quick review of each candidate's CV will allow you to ask specific questions, and it will make applicants feel that you're truly interested in them. When you want to attract the best people for the job, this will make a candidate more likely to accept your company's offer over another's.

If you're the interviewee, you have to make sure you have the opportunity to provide the most important information about yourself. Be sure to elaborate beyond your CV, and show your enthusiasm for your profession, as well as the opportunity to work for the company. If you have a tendency to ramble, the interview can be pulled into an unproductive direction. Prepare as much as possible, and write down answers to the questions you expect to be asked. Ask friends to tell you the questions they've been asked in interviews, and use their answers as a springboard to creating your own list of anticipated questions.

Make certain you understand what the organization's needs are, and then make sure you speak specifically to show how your knowledge, skills and experience add value. You cannot expect them to translate your background into their world. Employ comments such as: 'in the past I ...', 'currently I am ...', 'I mastered the use of ...'.

Improve Your Odds

Make an effort to connect with the interviewer. Look for 'free information': comment on photos, books, diplomas, trophies, wall hangings, or other aspects of the interviewer and his office that you can either identify with or show a sincere interest in. My friend Danielle Deutsch found this tip to be very useful. A recent graduate of the University of Michigan, she was being interviewed for her dream job at the American Civil Liberties Union offices in San Francisco. Thanks to Danielle's interest in art history, she commented on the piece of art being displayed as a screen saver on the decision maker's computer screen. This remark kicked off a lengthy conversation about their mutual passion for art. Rapport was instantly developed and Danielle landed her dream job.

Both the interviewer and interviewee need to listen carefully in order to keep the meeting focused. Sometimes, an interviewer is having a bad day and finding it hard to stay on point. In this case, you can, as the interviewee, find an opportunity to return the topic to yourself by saying something like, 'Another thing I'd like to tell you about is my experience at XYZ Corporation.' If you're the interviewer, it is your responsibility to bring a rambling interviewee back to the pertinent points. You can do this gently by simply saying, 'That's a great story, but I want to make sure I learn everything I need about you during our allotted time. Tell me more about your experience as a project coordinator.'

Staying focused in a confident talk conversation requires concentration, but the rewards are well worth the effort. You will not only accomplish your goals faster and more efficiently, but it's also one of the best ways to avoid unnecessary conflicts. When confident talk spins out of control, there are opportunities for miscommunication and chaos. Quite simply, chaos in business means a loss of efficiency, which will eventually turn into a loss in the bottom line. Staying organized and focusing your confident conversation is one of the most important things you can do to maintain healthy business relationships and healthy profits.

PUT COMPLAINTS ON THE RIGHT TRACK

Be careful when complaining to a special person in your life. Don't exaggerate. Victoria was used to using words such as 'always' and 'never', which were clearly exaggerations. Exaggerating helped Victoria let off steam, for sure. She often stated to her partner Ben that he 'never listened to her' and 'always forgot to look after the car service.' Nevertheless, by exaggerating her complaints, Victoria only succeeded in causing Ben to tune her out. 'I don't *always* do that,' Ben would think and sometimes say out loud, thereby convincing Victoria that she was, indeed, not being heard.

Best Practices

- Be genuinely concerned; give sincere and undivided attention to what you are being told.

- Take accurate notes to acknowledge that you are listening, and to address again at a later date.

- Identify misunderstandings calmly with friends and family, with love and empathy.

- Propose a resolution where possible.

- Summarize what you believe you heard to clarify meaning.

- Make a personal commitment to secure an agreed resolution—where possible.

- Define a resolution timeline and specific terms.

- Thank them for their time and input.

- Follow up on what was agreed.

4

USE SILENCE AS A TOOL

Learn why silence really is golden, especially in relationship building, negotiations, and presentations.

A speaker is introduced and walks out to the podium. The applause ends, but he doesn't speak—*not yet.* He stands quietly, making eye contact with various members of the audience. Everyone's attention is fixed on him as they anticipate his first words. This is the power of silence.

By taking advantage of these moments of quiet, the speaker has conveyed strength and confidence. He has commanded the room. But presentations are just one area where you can use silence to your advantage. It can be an equally effective tool in all sorts of conversations.

Any relationship will be enhanced when the power of silence is added to a conversation. The problem is that most of us feel awkward when a conversation appears to drop into the abyss. How do you react when this happens? Do you try to fill the quiet with whatever comes to mind? Do you squirm in your seat, hoping against hope the other person will say something … *anything?* If the silence follows something you've said, do you feel as if you did something wrong? On the other hand, do you still converse with your partner? Or are you like so many older couples—just stuck at the dining table in silence or with the TV or radio on, or both reading your sections of the newspaper? How many couples do we see eating out in public in complete silence? And *not* the comfortable silence of two old friends who are at peace with such quiet.

It can be useful to find out exactly how you feel when you're faced with silence. Ask someone to remain quiet with you for about 20 seconds. Does it seem like an eternity? Is it difficult to resist the urge to jump in and say something to fill the gap? If so, *breathe!*

It can be helpful to rehearse dealing with silences, especially if you find that your mind wanders and causes you to lose focus. Practise until you're comfortable with silences as long as 40 seconds. For most people, this feels like a very long time, but since most lulls in a conversation are shorter than 40 seconds, this practice will train you to be ready for anything. If you're prepared for it, silence can be your friend rather than an enemy.

We live in a noisy society, surrounded by external sounds, and many of us have become so accustomed to noise that we feel uncomfortable when there is a lack of sound, or, in conversation, when nobody is speaking. Many of us are, quite simply, uncomfortable with silence, and that's one reason why a lot of people have a television on, or radio, even when they hardly listen to it.

The truth is that when talking or listening, silence is helpful to allow both people to think. Understanding does not come automatically, but requires at least some degree of thought. A conversation with no gaps or silences doesn't allow people to process the information. What may be even worse is that we've become so uncomfortable with silence that we tend to prepare what we want to say while the other person is still talking, so as to fill in the anticipated gaps. That means we aren't listening. When communicating, most people underestimate the value of remaining quiet. In our rush to share our thoughts, we talk too much and sometimes interrupt the other person just to make sure our viewpoint is heard.

Two Tips to Increase the Quality of Your Conversations:

Ask a question and silently count to ten (or twenty if necessary):

Sometimes when posing a question, you feel at risk. If you do not get an immediate response, it's easy to want to explain yourself or rephrase your question. Instead of doing that, allow the person time to process what you've said and form their response.

Remain silent until the other person finishes speaking:

For some people, it feels impossible to do and yet it is priceless for improving communication and strengthening any relationship. Allowing someone to talk without interruption demonstrates that you value what they are saying. Being quiet shows respect for the person speaking. Respect increases the trust someone feels. Increased trust improves your relationship.

THE FIRST MEETING

Silences frequently happen immediately after you've been introduced to someone. Perhaps you have to walk down the hall from the reception area together before entering a meeting. While there's nothing wrong with the quiet that can naturally occur whilst queuing at the cinema, perusing a menu on a date, or taking a Sunday morning walk, these are also golden opportunities to begin building your relationship with this person. Confident conversation is taking the opportunity to get to know each other better, and it is up to us, not the other party, to take the lead. Use the silence to make a comment about what has been going on in your life, ask about a favourite film, or something interesting (but not controversial) that you read in the newspaper. Include an open-ended question that requires more than a 'yes' or 'no' response and you are sure to keep the conversation going.

Always make a second effort to keep a conversation going if your first attempt doesn't work. You may have simply focused on a subject that doesn't interest the other person. Don't be derailed by the lack of response, and move on to another topic.

Dealing with Unfriendly People

No matter how the other person responds, refuse to let yourself be thrown off balance. Most people are friendly and will gladly join you in conversation, but if you come across someone who refuses to be sociable, meeting your warmth with a wall of silence, don't take it personally. Maintain your equilibrium, and make the best of the situation.

THE ART OF THE QUIET NEGOTIATION

You've seen American films with actors like Al Pacino or Robert De Niro. The most intimidating man in the room is the one who can stay silent the longest while everyone else starts to squirm. While you shouldn't initiate a silence contest unless you have the confidence to pull it off, you need to be prepared when someone else instigates this kind of power play.

A silence contest generally begins when you ask the other person a question, and you're met with dead air. Such a contest is not for the faint of heart, and if someone decides to sit quietly for several seconds in an effort to watch you squirm, you know you're dealing with someone who wants to control you. In this situation, you have two choices—break the silence or try to win the contest. While it may be tempting to try to beat the other person at the game, it may not always pay off to be the most intimidating person in the room. Don't allow your sense of competition to get in the way of your objective. Instead, use the period of silence to genuinely contemplate what you have discussed. Then, interject a comment such as, 'After thinking about this further, I really believe it would be best to come to an agreement as to how best to divide household chores …' This should end the power play and get the conversation back on track.

Another important tactic is to simply *speak slowly.* This can be difficult when you have a lot to lose, but it's very important to leave plenty of gaps between your sentences. This allows the other party to jump in and make a concession, giving you the advantage. These small silences may throw the other person off balance enough so that they negotiate a point before you ask. For example, your son might assume your slow words are an indication that you're hesitating on a point. It might cause him to say, 'Well, if midnight is too late for you, how about 11:30?' If you pause after someone asks you something, they might even become so uncomfortable that they answer their own question. 'OK, Dad, how about we go with 11 o'clock curfew until I prove to you that you can trust me again?'

When you surrender to relevant pauses during a negotiation, you have the opportunity for productive listening. Observing and listening to the other people will help you adjust your responses based on their reactions. If you rush through the process, never allowing the quiet you need to assess the situation, you may miss important verbal and non-verbal cues … Rushing will cause you to talk *at* people, while taking time to breathe and observe will allow you to talk *to* and *with* people.

Slowing down and taking pauses gives you the time to read others and determine the best words and actions to reach your objectives.

IS SILENCE THE OPPOSITE OF SELLING?

You might think that silence during a sales call is the kiss of death, but top salespeople live by the motto that *less is more.* They know how to use silence to great advantage. If you get too wrapped up in your sales pitch, you may miss indicators from your prospect that they're ready to close the sale. If you miss that opportunity, the sale can quickly go up in smoke.

When you ask a closing question of your prospect, you must stop talking! This is especially true after you have offered your price or your deal. Ask, 'Can we agree on this price for the sound system?' and then do not allow another word to pass your lips! Your prospect will either be ready to close the sale or will raise an objection. Either way, this is when you need to listen. There may be a long pause while your prospect gathers his or her thoughts, but resist the urge to jump in with more sales talk that could only raise additional objections. If you have practised enough to become comfortable with 40 seconds of silence, you'll have no difficulty waiting for a decision.

You certainly don't want to become so vulnerable that you offer an unnecessary discount. This is a silence strategy used by some to get you to offer them your product or service for less. Try it sometime. If you're offered a certain amount of money to do a job, for example, stay quiet and see if the offer is increased.

Listening is important at the beginning of your sales call as well. Think how you feel when someone continues with their own agenda, oblivious to what you have just said. If a prospect has indicated that it isn't a good time, mention *in one sentence* the most important benefit of your product or service and ask when you could schedule a time to discuss what you have to offer. By being sensitive to your prospect's needs, you may just make the sale then and there.

Once you've made the sale and everyone has signed on the dotted line, you have another opportunity to practise some strategic silence. Be friendly, but don't wear out your welcome. Say thank you, and leave.

TAKING YOUR TIME IN AN INTERVIEW

Five seconds of silence during an interview can feel like an hour, but the more comfortable you are with pauses, the more confident you will appear. When an interviewer asks you a question, you're not expected to answer immediately. Taking a moment or two to gather your thoughts shows that you're contemplating the question in an effort to answer sincerely.

Some interviewers use silence as a tactical manoeuvre to see how well you handle stress. If you jump in too quickly, you run the risk of rambling until you're no longer saying anything relevant. The worst scenario is when you find yourself inadvertently revealing something negative about yourself just because you're intimidated by the gap in the conversation.

If an interviewer asks you a question, and your answer is met with a long silence, you can simply ask, 'Would you like to know more about that?' This brings the tactical manoeuvre back into your court. It's sort of like conversational tennis.

Active Listening

Don't forget to allow the interviewer to speak. Active listening helps to calm your nerves because it takes the focus off you and puts it on the other person. If you allow your anxiety to keep you focused on yourself, you might miss important cues from the interviewer that could help you adjust your approach and get the job.

If you want to feel at ease during your next interview, make sure you're well prepared. What are you likely to be asked? Don't forget to write down every question that comes to mind, and prepare your answers in advance. Keep your prepared answers to an appropriate length, however. If your answers are too short, it may look as if you have something to hide. If your answers are too long, you will appear nervous. Time yourself to keep your answers to no more than one or two minutes each.

If your nerves begin to get the best of you during a silence, whatever you do—remember to breathe and smile. If you hold your breath, the silence will feel longer, and your muscles will become tense.

POWERFUL PRESENTATIONS—IT'S ALL IN THE PAUSES

You can easily spot inexperienced public speakers. The adrenalin causes them to rush through the presentation, barely taking a breath. The audience struggles to keep up but eventually tunes the speaker out entirely. As Wolfgang Mozart said, 'The silences between the notes are as important as the notes themselves.' Without the silences in music, there would be no rhythm. Skilled speakers know how to use the blank spaces to create the same kind of drama as a concerto.

A few seconds of silence in a presentation can be effective for many reasons:

- When you want to emphasize something, stop to make your point. For example, you might offer a startling statistic such as, '85 per cent of the homes in this area are too expensive for 75 per cent of the population.' A pause after this statement will allow your audience to ponder its importance and will make the statistic all the more dramatic.

- If you say something funny, give the audience time to laugh!

- When a specific piece of information is complex, a few moments of silence will allow your audience to absorb what you have said.

- When you're shifting gears in your presentation, a slight pause will alert your audience that you're beginning a new point. It gives them time to digest what you have said before you offer the next bit of information.

Productive Pauses

'Umms' and 'errrs' are common communication fillers that get in the way of an otherwise good speech, negotiation, interview, networking interaction, or sales pitch. It seems to be human nature to fill gaps and lulls in conversation, and we rely on our own favourites to do so. Typical conversation fillers include 'you know', 'like', 'and stuff', 'I mean', 'or something', 'for the time being', 'basically', 'time and again', 'at the end of the day'.

Pausing is the best way to prevent habitually filling these lulls with fillers and to get over the 'umms' and 'errrs'. Pausing allows for well-timed speech and helps develop complete thoughts. Awareness of pausing is one thing—incorporating it is another. Pausing will help you project a more genuine and relaxed style.

Whenever you find your nerves getting the better of you, find a moment when you can pause to make eye contact with the audience. This will help you to feel that you're talking to individuals rather than a large intimidating group. It also allows you to make sure your audience is listening to you. If not, you may choose to switch gears by showing pictures or telling a story that will regain their attention.

Using silence effectively is an advanced communication skill. Observe others who use it well, and you'll learn a great deal. Practise staying quiet during silences in order to feel more comfortable. Soon, you'll stop feeling awkward and will smile quietly to yourself, waiting with confidence.

5

RECOGNIZE THE DANGER SIGNS

Identify confident conversation danger signs—stress, facial expressions, body language, and reactions to hot button topics—and discover how to send out positive conversational energy and keep from sending out negative energy.

In the American film, *Rounders*, Matt Damon's character plays poker with a big-time card sharp played by John Malkovich. Matt watches John's every move until he finally discovers Malkovich's 'tell'. Knowing this subtle body language allows Matt to win an enormous amount of money. Just like the characters in the film, the world's finest poker players have turned the study of body language into an art form. It's their bread and butter, and it can be yours, too.

According to psychologists, *what* you say only accounts for seven per cent of the impact you have on others. That leaves ninety-three per cent for *how* you say it, which includes your body language, your facial expressions, gestures, and the sound of your voice. No matter how great your information, if your presentation is lacking, you're plain out of luck.

You may have observed this problem in others. Have you

ever found yourself distrusting someone for no apparent reason? Body language was undoubtedly the culprit. If you don't understand what facial expressions and body language signify, you run the risk of making costly mistakes. When you study body language, you give yourself a substantial advantage in all of your dealings with people. You'll be able to read others to determine their underlying motives and whether they're telling the truth, and you'll be able to make sure you're presenting yourself in the best possible light, sending out positive energy.

Don't forget that body language is not an exact science, however. Certain gestures *generally* signify specific feelings in the majority of people, but you should use a variety of clues to read each person individually. For example, someone may be sitting in what would normally be construed as a closed posture with arms crossed. But it could be that this is the only comfortable way to sit in a particular chair. If the rest of this person's body language is very positive, such as leaning toward you and smiling sincerely, crossed arms may not be an indicator of anything negative.

PUTTING YOUR BEST FOOT FORWARD

You're probably unaware of what your body language conveys to others. What you don't know *can* hurt you, as you may be projecting an image that is counter to what you feel or what you want to present. If you want to come across as confident, honest, and knowledgeable (and who doesn't?), practise these steps until they feel natural to you. It can be helpful to videotape yourself to evaluate your unconscious body signals.

- **Eye contact.** Even if you find it uncomfortable to look others in the eye, train yourself to do it. Be careful not to stare, but looking into the eyes of others conveys self-confidence and shows that you're listening and engaged in the conversation. When you're speaking, however, use less eye contact. Looking into the eyes of your listeners too much will appear that you're demanding agreement. Dominating people do this, maintaining eye contact until the other person breaks it.

- **The handshake.** Keep your handshake firm, but not aggressive. If your handshake is too limp, you'll come across as insecure and passive, but if you squeeze too hard, you'll convey a desire to dominate. If you want to convey warmth, cover the handshake with your other hand.

- **Hold your head up.** Nod your head frequently to signify agreement, and vary your facial expressions in response to what is being said. Tilting your head sideways signifies interest, while lowering your head generally means you're suspicious of what you're hearing. If you want to convey a neutral attitude, keep your head centred.

- **Mirroring.** If it's a one-on-one meeting, mirror the other person's posture with yours. People feel comfortable with those who are like them, so gently mirroring the pose, tone, and facial expressions of the other person will put him or her at ease. Of course, keep it subtle. Don't change your pose every time the other person does so, and don't mirror someone who appears defensive. Conversely, when you notice someone mirroring your posture and gestures, it's a green light to make the sale or obtain agreement. Don't let that moment pass without asking for what you want.

Be reasonable about your mirroring, and, most importantly, sit or stand comfortably. No amount of mirroring will counter discomfort. Of course, if you're a man meeting with a woman, you won't cross your ankles to mirror her posture. If you're a woman meeting with a man, you may not be able to sit the same way as him, especially if you're wearing a dress. Crossed ankles are preferable for women, and one foot slightly in front of the other is best for men, perhaps with the toes of one foot touching the floor under the chair in what is termed the 'athletic position'.

- **Be still.** If your eyes wander, your foot swings, or your fingers drum, you'll give the impression that you're lying or, at the very least, not interested in the conversation. If your hands are very active or gripping your chair, you will project insecurity.

Don't fidget, but don't be rigid. Use gestures, but minimally.

- **Speak up.** Make sure you enunciate your words well and pronounce them correctly. Be careful not to speak too quickly. If you're uncertain about the speed of your speech, record yourself, or ask your colleagues and friends to give you an honest assessment.

- **Watch your posture.** Hold your shoulders erect, and don't slump. Good posture is a sign of confidence.

- **Keep your body language open.** Crossed legs are fine, but folded arms or hands in your pockets convey protectiveness. Keep your hands still and casual at your sides, in your lap, or on a table. To appear confident, place your hands in the 'steepling' position with the fingertips of one hand touching the fingertips of the other. If you want to convey your openness for negotiation, unbutton and/or remove your jacket in the presence of others. Open your palms to others often when you gesture, lean forward to show your interest, and touch your palm to your chest to signify sincerity when making a point. Be careful about appearing too casual, however. Leaning back in your chair

with your hands clasped behind your head may
even be taken as an arrogant stance.

NAVIGATING CULTURAL DIFFERENCES

The importance of facial expressions was in the news when Jack
Straw of the United Kingdom House of Commons requested
that Muslim women remove the veil worn over their faces.
Some Muslims were insulted by the request, but Mr. Straw felt
it necessary in order to truly communicate with the women.

Straw's request points to an important issue regarding
body language—*it isn't entirely universal.* Crossing your legs
may be fine in the western world, but pointing your toes at
someone in Thailand, for example, is considered rude. If you
practise your confident conversation in different cultures,
take the time to learn the customs as a gesture of your respect. People may forgive your faux pas, but you'll be accepted more quickly if you learn what is considered courteous
in the countries you visit. In Japan a nod doesn't mean agreement, instead it is a way to show concentration and attentive-
ness: closing the eyes in contemplation and a slight nod of
the head, up and down. If you're competing for business, taking the extra step to learn the various gestures, body language, and non-verbal communication will undoubtedly give
you the edge, particularly in Asia, where business people
spend a great deal of time studying body language.

KEEPING YOUR AUDIENCE AWAKE

When you're raising a glass to the bride and groom, giving a presentation to your garden club, having an important talk with your partner, whether at a podium, a conference table, a prospect's office, or your kitchen table, keep tabs on your listeners. Their body language will tell you a great deal about how you're doing and whether you need to make adjustments to maintain their interest. Here are some signs that your audience or sales prospect is bored or confused.

- Eyes are focused somewhere other than on you.

- Arms and legs are crossed in a defensive or protective posture.

- Mouths are closed tightly.

- Brows are furrowed or eyes are squinted.

- Fingers are running through hair.

If several of these signals occur, exaggerating your own body language is not the answer. You could certainly walk to the other side of the stage, causing your audience to follow you with their eyes, or you could raise your voice for dramatic effect, if it makes sense in the moment. This might be the perfect time to mention passionately a handy tip or statistic that affects your audience. One of the most dynamic ways to wake up someone across the table from you or when delivering a speech is to ask a question that evokes emotion. You might ask, 'Do you want to know the best way to kill your lavender plants, ladies and gentlemen? Once a plant is established, cut back on watering. Over-watering is one of the worst things you can do to your lavender plant.' Most importantly, make sure your voice and facial expressions are animated and passionate about your subject. Then, engage your audience in order to bring their attentions back to you.

In one-on-one discussions ask for her or his opinion. For example, you might be discussing your monthly budget. Ask specific questions in order to regain the attention of your partner. If you want to consider an expensive vacation, you might ask what current expenditures might have the best prospect of being cut without causing him or her too much stress. This would allow you to lead into your pitch your willingness to give up every other manicure or one weekly evening out with your friends. If it feels inappropriate to ask a question, reinforce why you believe what you are asking for is such a benefit: 'although more costly, this holiday package is a far better value because …'.

COOLING DOWN THOSE HOT BUTTONS

Everyone has 'hot buttons'—certain issues that trigger hurt feelings or anger. If you pay attention, however, you might be able to stop an argument before it begins.

What are the danger signs that signal you've hit a hot

button? You may experience these signs in yourself, or you may observe them in someone else—the clenched teeth, the furrowed brow, the raised voice, sweating, watery eyes, or redness in the face (which you will experience as heat). If you feel yourself becoming angry, take a few moments to cool off before you speak. It's much too easy to do damage to both business and personal relationships when your emotions have got the better of you.

When you find yourself confronted by someone who is very aggressive, using hostile communication tactics either consciously or unconsciously, do your best to stay calm. If you match the energy through word or body language, you'll only escalate the anger and keep the argument from reaching a resolution. This is a recipe for disaster, and it takes a great deal of control to prevent the other person's anger from affecting you. The natural inclination is to respond in kind in an attempt to protect yourself, but breathe and remind yourself that you'll be more protected if you're the one who keeps cool.

Avoiding the issue entirely, however, is also no solution. This generally leads to resentment from the other party and leaves the two of you walking on eggshells. You need to take a calm but proactive stance. It requires self-discipline to avoid reacting to the onslaught from the other person. Watch your own body language and try to relax your face as best you can. Avoid tight lips or crossed arms, which will only invite an adversarial response from the other party. Maintain an observer viewpoint, watching what is taking place with an objective, critical eye rather than an emotional one. Really listen to what the other person is saying rather than allowing the emotion to thrust you into a defensive position.

Defuse the emotion by remaining quiet at first, nodding in acknowledgement and tilting your head to signify that you're listening. Keep your body language receptive, opening your palms when you gesture. Turn your body slightly, which is a non-threatening posture, so that you aren't facing the other person directly. Resist the impulse to raise your voice or resort to finger pointing, reminding yourself that your side will be more likely to be heard when the situation is less heated.

Turning the Problem Around

When the conversation begins to calm down, you have the opportunity to redirect it more productively and positively. You might say, 'I would really like it if we could sit down and try to work this through together.' If the other person appears receptive, offer calming gestures such as a handshake or hand on the shoulder to signify your willingness to negotiate. If necessary, plan a meeting or getting together at a later time when you're both more likely to remain calm.

READING POKER FACES

Few people have the skill of an advanced poker player when it comes to deception. When the average person lies, he or she immediately becomes worried about getting caught. This causes stress that manifests itself physically. Below are some signals that someone may be lying, but be careful—they may also signify other emotions. Rather than jump to conclusions, stack the deck with several clues that the person may be trying to deceive you.

- The eyes are diverted from your gaze and may blink more frequently or dart around the room. Looking right while talking sometimes signifies dishonesty, while looking left is often an indication that what is being said is truthful.

- Breathing becomes heavier, and perspiration may occur.

- The voice goes into a higher pitch and/or becomes monotone. The liar may also stumble on his words.

- The body stiffens and/or the face tightens, especially the forehead and lips.

- Hands begin to fidget, perhaps rubbing together, scratching the nose, or covering the mouth. Palms may be turned down or hidden from view entirely.

- The body language closes up. Arms may be crossed or pulled into the sides of the body.

- Papers, cups, or other objects may be placed between the liar and others in the room as an unconscious barrier.

- The liar becomes suddenly still, waiting to see if you believe the lie.

What do you do if you suspect someone is lying? Move the conversation to a different subject as fast as possible, and watch the reaction of the potential liar. Does the person breathe more easily, or does he want to return to his subject? Liars are more likely to be relieved about a change of subject, while someone who is telling the truth will want to direct you back to the original conversation.

Whether you're trying to determine if someone is lying or attempting to make a big sale, body language is one of the most valuable tools you can learn for successful confident conversation. You can use it in every aspect of your life from interviews to board meetings to closing the biggest deal of your life.

6

IDENTIFY SOURCES OF CONFLICT

Identify potential sources of conflict, and demonstrate a willingness to explore all options.

Conflict is inevitable, but one thing is for sure—the better your ability to read body language and the better your confident conversation, the better chance you'll have of stopping conflict in its tracks. If you keep your eyes open for signs of trouble, you can often defuse a situation before it becomes damaging.

Whatever you do, don't ignore conflicts. Just like dirt swept under a rug, you'll eventually have to lift the rug and face the mess. And, inevitably, you'll find that the mess has grown while you were ignoring it. Conflict has a nasty habit of creating more damage when it has been left to fester. Again, communication is the key. This is as true in a corporation as it is in a marriage. After all, communication breakdown is what usually causes a conflict in the first place.

While you'll never avoid conflict entirely, there are certain precautions you can take to prevent problems from arising. Don't make assumptions about what people may already know. For example, a doctor shouldn't assume the pharmacist is giving his patients all of the information they need to administer their medicines properly. The only way to ward off future problems is to be explicit in your instructions and intentions.

Mind-reading

Watch for body language and non-verbal cues, but be careful about reading between the lines. When we attempt to read someone's mind, we're often wrong. For example, you may interpret your partner's anger as directed at you when he simply had a tough day at work. When in doubt about what someone is feeling or thinking, *ask.*

CONFLICTS WITH FAMILY

Family conflicts are as varied as the people involved in them. Turmoil can result from a workaholic husband whose wife feels lonely and resentful toward him, or children who are a source of continual family quarrels and frustration due to the parent's lack of time, outside stress, or inconsistent parenting skills. Blended families in which there is an unaccepted stepparent or interfering in-laws can be the source of family conflict. Every family has conflicts. In some families, differences and tension are a serious problem. In others, differences seem to be resolved fairly easily, without resulting in battles or horrible disputes. Think about the kinds of conflicts that happen in your family on a typical day. Conflicts over who should do what. For example, who should do the dishes? Who should be allowed to take the car on Saturday night? Who should stay at home when the kids are sick? Conflicts about how things should be done. For example, should home-work be done right after school or can it wait until after din-ner? Conflicts of personality and style. Mum thinks son John is too rough when wrestling with his younger brother. Dad thinks Mum should be more assertive with her friend but Mum prefers the soft approach.

PREVENT ESCALATION OF DISAGREEMENTS INTO ARGUMENTS AND MAJOR DISCORD

- Use I-statements rather than you-statements. They sound less accusing and place the responsibility for the statement on you. For example: 'I would like you to stack the newspapers for recycling before you leave,' *not* 'You need to stack the newspapers for recycling before you leave.'

- Steer clear of name-calling and put-downs. They are inflammatory and only make the other person defensive and angry, thereby escalating the conflict.

- Soften your tone. Listen to how you sound. A softer, friendlier tone of voice helps lessen the hostility of your message.

- Take a time-out. Some families have an agreement to make the time-out sign (make a 'T' with your hands) when a discussion escalates into an argument. Say, 'Let's take a break and cool down, and agree on how long the time-out should be. We can resume this conversation where we left off when the time is up.'

- Acknowledge the other person's point of view. It is not necessary to agree. For example: 'I hear what you are saying,' *or* 'I accept that you think you did the right thing.'

- Watch your language. Use specific words and facts. Stay away from generalities. For example: 'You were an hour late,' *not* 'You're always late,' *or* 'I can never count on you.'

Think of situations in your life in which conflicts do not occur. What might be happening in these situations? Chances are you are practising one of the following conflict-prevention skills:

- Address issues before they become problems. For example, if you know that you need to attend a business dinner next Tuesday evening, talk to your partner about it now and ask him/her to be home early to feed the kids. Don't wait until the last minute.

- Be aware of triggers. For example, your teen's lack of eye contact makes you upset. During a calm moment, talk to him/her about it. Explain that it triggers your anger, and ask him/her to try to look at you when you are having serious discussions. When he/she does, praise the improvement.

- Have a process for resolving conflicts. During a calm moment, discuss the process with your family and get agreement on what members should do when there are differing viewpoints.

- Remove the word 'but' from your vocabulary. When you say it, you cancel out everything before the 'but'. You also cancel an apology on your part when you state a reason—after the 'but'—for doing whatever you did. For example: 'I'm sorry for yelling but if you weren't so aggravating I wouldn't have to yell.' In this instance, the key is to apologize for your own behaviour, rather than coupling your apology—and crippling it—with an accusation.

CONFLICTS ON THE JOB

When two employees are having difficulty with one another, you may be called upon to act as a kind of mediator. Emotions are often running high in these situations, and the more calm and objective you remain, the more likely it is that you will be able to defuse the anger.

Interview each party separately at first in order to understand the specifics of the conflict. Listen to them carefully with respect, empathy, and without interruption, allowing them to vent, if necessary. This will dissipate the emotions, as each person will feel heard. Ask each of them to describe their expectations and how they feel the situation is unfair. You might also ask them to tell you their definitions of 'fair', as these will vary from one person to the next. Recognize that both parties have perceived the same situation differently, and neither of their positions can be taken as fact.

Encourage the free expression of feelings in your individual meetings with the parties. Sometimes, people simply push each other's buttons, and deep-seated issues come to the surface that actually have little to do with the situation itself. If you can determine the vulnerability or fear under the anger, you may be able to dissipate their defences and get to the heart of the matter. Be careful not to embarrass or expose anyone, however. Deep-seated issues can be delicate and very private matters that go back to childhood. Such disclosures are best left out of the workplace.

When and if it becomes necessary to hold a meeting with

both parties together, state the positions of each person objectively, without accusing either party. For example, you might say, 'Joe, I understand that you felt you weren't receiving enough support in your tasks. Am I right?' To the other party, you might say, 'Allison, I understand that you felt it would have been infringing on Joe's turf if you offered that support without being asked. Is my understanding correct?' Often, if you state the positions of each person in a calm and simple way without accusation, you can begin to find solutions to the problem. You are acting as the communicator in a situation where communication has broken down. When people feel unheard, hurt feelings and defensiveness may prevent them from speaking to each other effectively. An objective third party may be all that's required to cut through the miscommunication.

Ask each person to think creatively about how the situation can be improved, even if they think everything is the other person's fault. Try to determine if there are common interests and goals shared by both parties, and keep your focus on solving the problem at hand, not fixing the people involved. Again, think *problem-oriented talk*, not *person-oriented talk.* Try to get both parties to work together to find a better way of dealing with the problem.

When two employees simply cannot get along but must work together, spend time with them to discuss how they can each focus on their common goal rather than their personality conflict. Ask them to think of creative ways they might resolve to work together despite the problems. Perhaps they can 'agree to disagree' and avoid difficult subjects with one another.

Conflicts Between You and an Employee

When you sense a conflict or problem developing between you and an employee, address it early before it escalates. The longer you let the situation go on, the more difficult it will be to resolve. Work hard to understand your employee's feelings and point of view. Before forming an opinion about an employee's action you need to hear the other side of the story. For example, 'Mrs. Lewis in room 401 complained to me about your conduct with her. Obviously, I wasn't there, so I'd like to hear what took place from you. And then let's figure out what can be done to resolve it.' Stay calm, and offer *validating talk*. Repeat back what you believe you heard so that your employee realizes you genuinely care. 'As I have been listening to you, I have the sense that you are frustrated with the resources available to you. Is that correct?' Be firm yet positive whenever possible, you certainly don't want to cower and allow an employee to walk all over you, but the more you listen, the more you will be able to avoid future conflict, even if you must say no to your employee's request. 'Unfortunately, because of current economic conditions, it is not possible to give you a raise at the present time.' If the response is, 'If not now, when?' and you do not know, say, 'I can't say. We'll have to see how things go,' or 'I'm sorry, I am not certain what you can expect.' If the pressure is on for an immediate answer and you do not want to be rushed, say, 'If you need an answer right now, the answer is no.' If you are not certain, use the words 'not now' or 'not at the present time'. Saying 'not

---

Conflicts Between You and an Employee

---

now' and changing your answer to 'yes' is far easier than saying 'yes' and later changing your answer to 'no'. And if used truthfully, 'not now' takes the sting out of 'no'.

Below are some guidelines to prevent the breakdown of communication that so often results in conflict.

- Make sure everyone involved is informed about matters that concern them.

- Identify your goal for the relationship, or a project, and clarify the role that each person will play, as well as what is expected of each of the people involved.

- Think carefully about the personalities of the people involved. Are you asking your disorganized and overwhelmed friend to manage small details for a party that may be a more appropriate role for you or someone else to play? Has she let you down previously when it came to significant details? When working with a group consider which personalities are most likely to work well together.

- Brainstorm alternatives to potential problems.

- Try resolutions on for size. Ask him or her to try a new strategy to discover what works. Give it a set period of time as a trial; ask for cooperation and it will be easier to convince them if it's only for a trial period. Once the trial period is over ask for feedback. People who were once in conflict may just begin working together toward a common goal.

NEGOTIATION REQUIRES YOUR MOST CONFIDENT STYLE

Before you sit down to begin negotiating with someone—whether a business associate or a family member—you need to ask yourself a very important question: *How much is at stake?* If you never expect to deal with these people again, you can refuse to give in, pushing your agenda as far as you like to win your objective. When you will continue to have dealings with the people involved, however, negotiation becomes a subtle art that requires finesse.

Of course, finesse doesn't mean you should resort to manipulations or try to trick the other party into losing out. Honest and fair diplomacy is what is required to resolve problems—either during or after your deal. In other words, *confident conversation.* Both parties need to win on a few points and lose on a few points in order to maintain the relationship. Compromise is absolutely necessary on both sides, or the end result will be a breakdown of trust and a breakdown of the relationship. (Be careful not to resort to 'haggling', however, as this is more likely to lead to an adversarial relationship than a compromise.)

Ideally, both sides of the argument should leave the exchange feeling that they each received *most* of what they wanted. Strive to come to an agreement that actually strengthens the relationship, not weakens it. Now, that's confident talk indeed, but it isn't as difficult as you think. You simply need to lay the groundwork before you begin the conversation. If you take the time to think about all of the different aspects of the situation, you'll be armed with bargaining chips and able to anticipate some of the problems before they arise.

Many family and relationship situations require negotiating with others. Deciding which restaurant to dine at, when to move to a new home, planning how to spend money, choosing a holiday destination, and many other decisions work best when you learn to negotiate with tact.

Negotiation skills increase your personal effectiveness in any group situation—volunteer groups, charity events, church, mosque, or synagogue groups, for example.

- Successful negotiators make a plan, they take the time to analyse the situation and think through their strategy.

Example. Michael wants to begin jogging again to get into better physical shape. He became a new father six months ago and has had no time to exercise. He anticipates that Jenna, his wife, will resist any talk of his wanting to take time for himself, since the responsibilities of parenthood are so time consuming. For a while, he avoids the subject, fearing that it will turn into an argument. Then, he starts to feel angry and resentful. He decides to negotiate with Jenna and begins by making a list of his needs and wants, as well as her needs and wants.

• Successful negotiators are willing to consider a wide range of outcomes and options rather than rigidly insisting on a specific result. They are open minded and avoid being locked in to one outcome. They are willing to consider many possibilities and combinations of options.

Example. Lucy is feeling very stressed by the long commute to her job. She was thinking of resigning until she decided to make a list of other options. She came up with several alternatives—working from home two days a week, working part-time rather than full-time, working flexible hours to avoid rush-hour traffic, and working from home every fourth week.

• Successful negotiators look for common ground rather than areas of conflict. They point out areas where he/she and the other person are already in agreement. Doing so conveys an attitude of cooperation and lessens any feeling of opposition.

Example. Laura wants her next car to be a Volvo because of its reputation for safety. Harry, her husband, wants a sports car. She says to Harry, 'Let's talk about what we agree on. First, we both agree that the car has to have a strong safety record. Second, we want to buy a new car, not a used one like last time. And third, we've set our price range as thirty thousand pounds or less.'

• Successful negotiators discuss the key issues in order of priority. They have a clear idea of what the two or three key issues are and which is the most important. They start with the most important issues and proceed to those that matter less. If they can reach agreement on the most important things, the lesser issues will most likely be easier to resolve.

Example. Carol wants her next family vacation to be something really special—either a Caribbean cruise or a trip to Latin America. She and her family have visited relatives or stayed at home for the past few years. She wants the family to have an experience they will always remember before Geoff, their adolescent son, moves away. She sees the key issues as follows:

☐ There are only three years left before Geoff leaves. He is not likely to join us for a vacation after he finishes school.

☐ It is important to have an exceptional vacation at least once in your life.

☐ If we plan ahead and save the money, we will be able to afford the cost of such a trip.

Two Different Scenarios

Scenario One:

Jon: 'I can't believe you are being so rigid.'

Kristina: 'Rigid! You should talk! You are completely bull-headed.'

Jon: 'Right! You should try listening to yourself. You are impossible.'

Scenario Two:

Jon: 'I can't believe you are being so rigid.'

Kristina: 'You're not happy with what I've asked for.'

Jon: 'You're damn right! You have to consider what I want.'

Kristina: 'Tell me more about it, then. I'll be happy to listen.'

In Scenario One, Jon and Kristina dig themselves in deeper with each statement. In example Two, Kristina blocks

---

Two Different Scenarios

the discussion from spiralling out of control and makes it possible for communication to resume. With practice, you can learn to use these simple skills to get more of what you want in life—without coming across like a bully. In fact, these skills help you reach agreements that are more likely to satisfy both parties while they maintain a positive relationship.

PREPARING FOR YOUR OWN NEGOTIATION

If a major disagreement is involved, you should prepare thoroughly for the conversation. It will allow you to clarify your own position, as well as put yourself in the shoes of the other party. Use the worksheet below to ask yourself the right questions.

NEGOTIATION WORKSHEET

1. What is at stake? How important is it that you and the other party come to an agreement?

_____

_____

2. In what ways are you and the other party already in agreement? Consider beginning your meeting by reiterating these points to establish goodwill.

_____

_____

3. What do you want in this situation?

_____

_____

4. What do you believe the other party wants in this situation?

_____

_____

5. What can you offer the other party as a trade in order to get more of what you want?

_____

_____

6. What can you ask the other party for as a trade in order to offer something they want?

_____

_____

7. What are you prepared to give away, and in what ways are you prepared to compromise?

_____

_____

8. What is absolutely not negotiable from your point of view?

_____

_____

9. Where does the power lie in your relationship with the other party? Who controls what?

_____

_____

10. Will your relationship with this person in the past affect your ability to reach an agreement? Are there unresolved personality or historical issues that might come into play?

_____

_____

11. If there are past issues, what strategies can you use to soften these problems and keep them out of the current negotiation?

_____

_____

12. If an agreement cannot be reached, what are the consequences to you personally and professionally?

_____

_____

13. If an agreement cannot be reached, are there alternatives or options for resolving the situation?

_____

_____

14. Are there others in your organization with expectations as to the outcome? If so, what are those expectations? What are the consequences to them if you cannot reach an agreement?

_____

_____

TACKLE PROBLEMS NOT PEOPLE

Guard against taking anything personally when you're involved in a negotiation, and strive to prevent others from doing so as well ... Avoid blaming, even if others in the exchange resort to it. Your negotiation skills are required to an even greater degree when the people you're dealing with have few skills in this area.

When the other party or parties resort to manipulation or try to force you into a win–lose situation, gently rebuke them for their tactics. You might simply say, 'It's counter-productive to avoid any kind of compromise.' Then, look for the common ground between you. Try to find where your interests are the same in order to create camaraderie, rather than conflict. In all conflicts, tackle the problem, not the people involved. The more you focus on the task at hand, the more likely it is that everyone involved will be able to work together toward a solution.

Of course, when compromise fails to work and one side must win while the other loses, some compensation must be given in order to maintain the relationship between you. In this way, you can turn a win–lose result into a win–win.

CONFLICT CHART

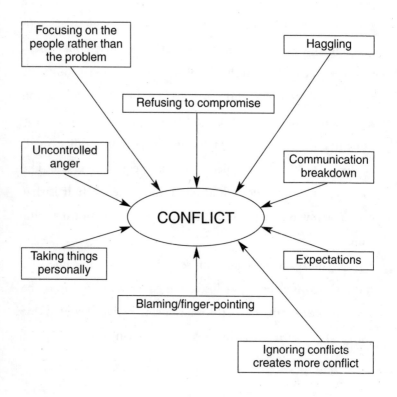

AVOIDING/RESOLVING CONFLICT CHART

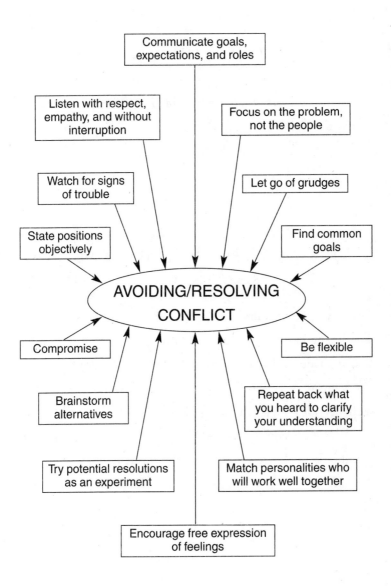

7

Improve Your Timing

Recognize how timing plays a critical role in all of your personal and professional communication, from asking for a pay rise, to talking about your feelings.

PERSONAL RELATIONSHIPS REQUIRE SPECIAL TIMING

When you go on a first date, you don't start by talking about how many children you would have together. The day after you've made a sale, you don't call your customer to find out if she wants to place another order. 'Timing is everything' may be a cliché, but it's a truth that applies in every aspect of life.

I have already discussed the importance of starting with small talk, but there are more subtle timing issues with regard to confident talk that can sometimes make or break a relationship or a deal.

ASKING FOR A DATE

When asking somebody out on a date, timing is everything. You need to make sure that you ask the person out at the appropriate time. If you do not you may end up embarrassing yourself or, even worse, the other person.

When asking somebody out, never do it around other people. There is no need to have a group of friends with you when you are going to ask somebody out on a date. In the same way, it is inappropriate to ask out somebody who is standing in a crowd. Simply wait until you can get the person alone, or if you must, you can slyly ask to speak to them in private.

So, choose your moments wisely and make sure you are taking advantage of your best opportunity.

What Can You Do to Make an End-of-the-day Chat Ritual?

Partners living together are faced with the prospect of staying connected at the end of their respective days. What is the best time—riding home from work, while cooking, after dinner, later in the evening? How can you make it comfortable for both people? A partner who loves to be busy may want to chop vegetables while talking. A partner who is physically exhausted may want to put his or her feet up and enjoy a comfortable chair while talking. Work together to build a talk-time ritual that strengthens your relationship.

LET'S TALK 'ABOUT US' CONVERSATION

Maybe you have been dating for a while, which is a time frame that may mean two months to some and two years to others. We all know it's coming. It's the 'let's talk about us' conversation. It's as certain as death and taxes and sometimes just as painful. In order to ensure you get through the conversation, you have to consider when to have it, how to have it and what to do if things go bad. Let's take a look at what's involved in 'the conversation'.

Timing is crucial. Although there are no set rules, the first date is never the right time for a chat of this magnitude—and this is even if you have spent three entire days of non-stop talking, amazing chemistry, and romance the rest of us can only imagine. You need time to get away and reflect because it's very easy to get swept up in the passion of a new relationship. A good idea is to make sure you get the big conversations out of the way, such as what you want out of your life. If you want to have children and they don't, it might be better to call it a night. However, if you want four and they only want two, perhaps there's some middle ground you can work on. If you want to move to Antarctica and they're allergic to snow, that's also a good time to wave the waiter over for the bill. Conversations like these can go on for hours or days, but you want to make sure you take the time to have them before you sit down for 'the big one'.

The conversation should never begin with 'I think we need to have a talk.' At best, it strikes fear into the hearts of even those who were hoping to have the same talk with you. At worst, it's a cliché. To start out by asking them where they think the relationship is at, is backhanded, will be perceived as a game, and could easily backfire. All that you really can and should do is sense the right moment in a conversation, and then tell the other person how you feel when you are together and then where you think you'd like to be going. With any luck, there will be agreement and all the good things you have mentioned will surely make the moment right. In case you don't get the response you're looking for, you might not want to do it in public ...

Unfortunately, sometimes the two of you just aren't headed in the same direction. Be as prepared as possible for a response that is not the one you would have liked. What do you do if someone drops 'the conversation' on you? Obviously, it is impossible to prepare for something like this; all you can do is speak from your heart. If you speak the truth and don't try and hide anything, it will come across in the best way you could ever hope. If you try and beat around the bush or flat out lie, odds are the issue will not be resolved.

The conversation is just that: two people together discussing where they are in life and in love. It's a necessary part of any growing relationship and you'll have many of them over your time together. Just remember that these talks are vital to a great relationship and ensure you're spending time with the right type of person for you.

TIMING CONVERSATION WITH CHILDREN

Any parent will tell you that 'real' conversation with a child can grow more difficult as they do. Just this year a mum who had newly been transferred by her company described her cure for the silent treatment from her seven-year-old son. She had uprooted her boy from his home town, the only place he had known and left behind his friends, school mates and even grandparents. Each day after school she enquired: 'How was school?' Mum could not get more than a one-word answer out of him: 'Fine'. She was concerned that he was miserable about the move and was desperate for open communication between her and her son. Luckily for her, the boy longed for the newest video gizmo. At her wits' end one day she offered: 'Son, I will give you one pound for each time you give me a real answer of at least a full sentence to my question asking how you are.' He was full of information after that. A bribe is certainly a consideration but the following might be better times to take on conversation with children:

IN THE CAR

Nothing like a captive audience to get a conversation going. Your child might also appreciate the ability to talk to you without actually having to look at you or make eye contact. Keep your eyes on the road, and your ears open.

BEGINNING OF THE DAY

If your child is a morning person, haul yourself out of bed in those early hours too and share some a.m. time together. You may find your child to be more open before all the daily hassles and attitude have been layered on.

BEFORE BED

Turning out the lights sometimes brings out thoughts and feelings that are too scary for daytime. Be available to sit with your child and talk a little after bedtime but before sleep. It's a good time to catch your child with his or her guard down.

ON AN AFTERNOON OUT

Every now and then, plan a little outing with just you and your child. Maybe go to a shop he or she particularly likes and have a treat, or stop for a cup of coffee and a cookie at a bookshop or café. Be a couple of friends, visiting and talking.

ON A WALK

Grab your child for a stroll around the block, or walk to a local shop instead of driving. Walking a pet also provides a good opportunity for an informal chat. Get fit and get informed at the same time.

WHILE YOU'RE WAITING

In a doctor's waiting room, queuing in a shop, in traffic, wherever you're sitting with your child with time on your hands, take up the opportunity to talk a little. You may have to yank the iPod earphones from those young ears, but give it a try.

ON A BREAK

If your child's working on a tough homework assignment, schedule a little break for a cold drink, a stretch, and a short conversation. Either a break from work will be an incentive for your child to talk, or having to talk will be incentive to get back to work!

WHILE WATCHING TELEVISION

TV gives you a nice break sometimes, but watching it with your child can also be helpful if it gives you some prompts for conversation starters. Ask your child if the events or the characters or the feelings you're viewing remind him or her of anything that's going on for real.

ANY TIME AND ALL THE TIME

The best way to get your child to talk to you is just to be open and available for talk all the time. Let your child know you enjoy his or her company and conversation, whether there's something important to discuss or you're just wondering about the weather. Hey, it wouldn't hurt to learn how to IM (instant message) or text message, either.

Sometimes the most powerful parent–child conversations take place while the two of you are doing something else. Kids tend to be more comfortable if they don't have to look at you directly while they're talking about important issues. Here are a few places and ways to talk about not smoking, for example, so that kids can make the right decisions:

- Choose your timing wisely, we all have things in our minds, so get into the habit of checking with the other person to see if the timing is right.

- Have your important discussions earlier rather than waiting until the last minute when it might be too late to address an issue or too emotionally charged. In other words, get into the habit of not letting things that bother you fester. Think about it as a wound. Unless you take care of it immediately, it will be much harder (or messier) to treat after some time.

- Stop the conversation if you find yourself being distracted, need to leave, or it gets out of hand. Resuming your talk later is better than being rushed or regretting something you might say but not mean.

TIMING MEANS BUSINESS

As important as timing is in our personal life, timing can mean winning or losing an account, getting a raise, or keeping a customer.

Timing in Marketing Strategies

If you bombard your customers with marketing materials, you're likely to lose them forever. On the other hand, if you fail to keep your company's name in their minds, they may take their business elsewhere. Striking a balance can be a complex dance, but the more you know, the better you will be able to time your marketing efforts appropriately.

If you operate a gift hamper business, for example, your customers would no doubt appreciate reminders before holidays such as Mother's Day and Valentine's Day, which include gift ideas and special ways to appreciate their loved ones. The timing of these messages makes sense, and they're actually helpful to your customers. Sending Christmas gift ideas every month of the year, however, is another story. For example, you probably hate getting those magazine subscription renewal reminders two months after you have started your subscription. Imagine yourself in your customer's position, and think about how you would experience your sales messages.

For 'evergreen' businesses such as the insurance industry, learn all you can about your target market to determine when your potential customers would be most likely to buy what you're selling. Your industry may maintain a seasonal or fiscal schedule that will make customers more receptive at certain times of the year, or you may discover that a particular customer maintains an in-house schedule that will make your well-intentioned messages unwelcome during certain months.

When determining how often and when to send marketing materials, stop to think about what you want to accomplish. Are you trying to sell as much of a specific product as you can *right now*, or are you trying to develop trust for the long term? For quick sales, short flyers, emails, or postcards may do the trick. For building relationships, offer your customer something of value to accompany a reminder about your services. This could be a special sale for long-time customers or a discount for a period of time. When you're dealing with an individual, consider keeping track of birthdays and sending cards in order to establish goodwill.

No matter what your industry, if your sales pitch accompanies information that your customers can use, the response will be more receptive. If you send sales letters that contain nothing of value, your customers are likely to become annoyed—especially if your messages arrive too frequently. The last thing you want is to be pegged as a spammer! Include articles or tips with your marketing materials, and your customers will appreciate and look forward to receiving them. Newsletters, for example, are an excellent way to remain in your customers' minds. This will establish goodwill and show that you genuinely care about your clients. Just make sure that you include articles that are truly useful.

TIMING IN SALES CALLS

When you arrive for an unscheduled one-on-one sales call, be sensitive to the possibility that your prospect may be too busy to speak to you. Use the moment to find out the best time to continue the conversation, and take your leave before you wear out your welcome. Most importantly, don't expect a sale sooner than your target market allows. Some organizations won't buy until a series of steps have been completed, and final decisions are often made by a committee. Learn your market's protocols and cycles, or you could quickly turn off your prospects and lose sales.

Learning about personality types is also crucial in order to assess your customers and determine how best to communicate with them. Some people like a great deal of small talk before getting to the confident talk regarding your product or service. Others prefer to get right down to business, hearing immediately what you have to offer. In fact, these types will become downright annoyed if you engage in too much small talk. The better you develop your ability to recognize someone's preferred conversational style, the better you will time your movement from small talk to confident talk.

If you sense your prospect is reluctant to buy, ask open-ended questions that require more than a yes or no answer, such as 'What do you think of this feature?' When you know your prospect's reservations, you can counteract them with additional information.

If, on the other hand, you sense that your prospect may be

ready to buy, ask a question that requires a yes or no answer, such as 'Do you see how my product could help you save money?' If you receive a 'yes' answer, you know it's time to ask for the sale. If you receive a 'no' answer, you know that you need to present more convincing evidence.

Always remain mindful of the amount of time you're taking with a prospect, and keep your questions to a minimum. If your efforts seem to be promising but not yet leading to a sale, ask if you can send additional information or make another appointment to speak with the person again.

If you're a sales manager, you may have occasion to accompany one of your salespeople on a call. On these occasions, keep in mind that this is not your territory. You are there to observe, not take over. Allow your salesperson to do his or her job, and resist the urge to jump in and make the pitch yourself. Not only is it the courteous thing to do, but it will allow you to observe the salesperson's work. Only then will you be able to offer specific feedback. Obviously, if the call nears the end and is not going well, you can jump in and save it. This will give you the opportunity to demonstrate your expertise for your salesperson's benefit and help close the sale.

Mealtime Etiquette

Etiquette experts agree:

- At breakfast, business conversation can commence when the coffee is poured.

- At lunch, make small talk until ordering, and then talk business.

- At dinner, the host should introduce business into the conversation.

TIMING IN PRESENTATIONS

Remember the power of silence in a speech—taking a moment to pause for dramatic effect? This is only one way in which timing plays an important role during a speech or presentation. First of all, the length of time you choose to speak is vital to how well you're received. If you speak for too long, you will soon be talking to yourself while your audience is off in their minds thinking about shopping lists or problems with spouses.

Try not to cram too much information into your presentation. Think carefully about how much your audience will be able to absorb in one sitting and the amount of information they expect to receive. Even if you're the greatest speaker in the world, no one will want to listen to you all day. Time yourself during practice sessions to make sure you don't go over your allotted time, but bear in mind that rehearsals take approximately twenty-five per cent less time than the actual performance. Therefore, be sure to practise at a slow pace. Research shows that people can take in less than 150 words per minute, so try to plan your time with the audience's comprehension speed in mind.

Time each section of your speech to make sure you don't stay on one aspect of your topic for too long. Cover the pertinent information, and move on to your next point in order to make all of your points during your allotted time. For each fifteen minutes of your speech, plan on engaging your audience by asking them a question or showing a PowerPoint slide containing a picture or graph. If you pose a question, you can ask something hypothetical that doesn't require a verbal response. Simply asking the question will return any wandering minds to your subject as everyone thinks about their responses and becomes engaged in your speech.

It's almost inevitable that you'll end up running out of time, so don't save your best material for the end of your speech. Certainly prepare a great ending, but start off with some of your most exciting information. Otherwise, you may end up having to rush through it at the end. If you have to announce that you're unable to show some slides that were promised because you've run out of time, your audience will lose faith in you. The best way to avoid this is to keep a watch or small clock where you can see it (but out of view of the audience, if possible) to make sure that you time each section of your speech appropriately. This should help prevent a mad rush at the finish and keep you on track throughout your speech. Don't wear your watch on your wrist, however, as your audience will see you looking at it and become distracted.

TIMING IN MEETINGS

Everyone's time is valuable, and if you plan too many meetings that prove to be unproductive, people will resent it. This means that you must not only plan your meetings carefully, but you must require that everyone be on time. If you constantly wait for latecomers, those who have arrived on time will feel disregarded. When the chronically late miss the beginning of enough meetings, they will no doubt begin to arrive on time.

Remain equally as vigilant about the time you end the meeting. It's the only way for everyone to keep a schedule, and they will appreciate that you respect their time. When the ending time arrives, schedule another meeting to finish your agenda, if necessary.

TIMING AND YOUR BOSS

If your timing is off when you ask for a raise or present an idea to your boss, you're wasting your breath. Before you decide to make a request of a supervisor or manager, consider his or her schedule and current circumstances. Monday mornings and Friday afternoons are generally poor times for such discussions. If your boss has many meetings scheduled, a big project due, or just appears to be irritable, bide your time. Of course, if you have no way of knowing your boss's schedule, simply say, 'I'd like to talk to you about an idea I have. Is this a good time, or would you like to schedule something later?'

When asking for a raise, take your organization's performance review schedule into account. If you have just completed a glowing project or have been given new responsibilities, don't wait for your review in six months. Take advantage of the fact that your success is fresh in your supervisor's mind. If your review is only two weeks away, however, wait until just before that time to ask for the raise. Since your review is more about finding out what you might be doing *wrong*, it doesn't hurt to alert your boss to what you're doing *right* just prior to the time of your review.

Never ask for a raise, of course, when you know the company is going through financial difficulties. You're unlikely to be successful, and you will only undermine your efforts in the future. See Chapter 12 for more tips about asking for a raise or promotion.

When you're changing jobs, negotiate a higher salary after the position has been offered but before you have formally accepted it. This is the time when you have the most leverage. You can even let the employer know that you have another offer (if you do) or say you'd like to think about it. They just may make a higher offer to coerce you to make an immediate decision. Don't take too long to give them an answer, though. If your initial counter-offer is rejected, try to negotiate a guaranteed increase after a few months within the company. Never allow it to be stipulated that you only receive the raise if your performance is satisfactory, however, because this is a judgement call that can easily be used against you.

Dealing with the Difficult Boss

If your boss is difficult to deal with, he or she may fall into one or more of many different categories: bullying, incompetent, tyrannical, indecisive, or just plain nasty.

There are tactics that can help advance a resolution. Present ideas not as 'Here's what I want,' but as 'Here's how I can help you.' Use an advocate approach; for example, say to your boss, 'I've been wondering if you would think about helping us work together better.' An advocate approach gives direction to the conversation while allowing the boss to take the bull by the horns.

It is awfully difficult for a boss to argue with a comment like: 'When you ask me to design prototypes at the last minute, it is very difficult to do my best work ... I'd like to spend more time on research in order to come up with a more complete plan. With more notice, I think I could improve what we deliver to the customer.' The impatient, disorganized boss ought to be asked, 'What do you need me to finish next?' rather than 'What do you need me to start next?'

Dealing with the Difficult Boss

Ask for a meeting. Say, 'I'd like to meet with you this week to discuss some ideas I have about how we can work more efficiently. Would Tuesday be a good day?' Who can say 'no' to that?! Avoid using defensive phrases such as, 'you may not recognize ...' or, 'you may not be aware ...' or, 'you may not mean to ...'.

Be wary of the hastily written angry email. It can lead to disaster as it cannot be recalled after real damage is done.

TIMING AND CONFLICT

The biggest problem when it comes to conflict is trying to resolve it too soon when emotions are too hot. When you attempt to make your points before both of you have cooled down, you will only make matters worse. If someone else tries to press you before you feel you can communicate rationally, be firm about asking for more time. Learn your own limits, and never allow yourself to be pulled into an argument before you're ready to speak from a less emotional place.

If an argument does get out of hand, be willing to call a 'time-out', but don't use this as a way out of the discussion. Be sure to genuinely work on calming yourself, so that you can come together for a discussion as soon as possible. If you wait too long to resolve problems, they become like sore shoulders in the relationship. You may be able to ignore the pain, but it's still there. And if you leave too many issues unresolved, the pain will eventually become unbearable.

Of course, resolution doesn't always mean that you come to an agreement. It simply means that you come to some sort of understanding with one another, which may involve agreeing to disagree. The ultimate goal is for each party to feel safe with the other person—whether in a personal or business relationship. If each of you manages to respect the other's point of view, the relationship can continue harmoniously.

Timing is an advanced skill that requires finesse and sensitivity. The more you cultivate your ability to assess personality types, read body language, and put yourself in another person's shoes, the better your timing will become. You'll never read other people with one hundred per cent accuracy, but you can significantly reduce your margin of error with a little bit of effort and knowledge.

8

_____

SEND OUT POSITIVE ENERGY

Discover how to send out positive conversational energy and keep
from sending out negative energy.

You walk into a room full of people, and you don't know a soul. You scan each corner, looking for someone who appears to be approachable. Some people may cause you to feel unwelcome, while others draw you toward them magnetically, making you feel eager to start a conversation. The people you instinctively want to approach are sending out positive energy, while there is something amiss about the people who make you feel uncomfortable.

What kind of energy do *you* send out? You may be a great confident talker, but if the energy you convey is negative or awkward, your words will fall flat. So, how can you be one of the people who put out positive energy and draw others to you? It simply takes some awareness to make sure you are presenting yourself in an upbeat, confident way. When you take the time to examine what you do in confident talk situations, you will be able to make adjustments to alter the energy that others feel from you. The more positive you are, the faster you will cultivate trust and rapport in both business and social circumstances. Remember that everyone knows an average of over two hundred people. You never know the advantageous connections you can make if your energy pulls people toward you.

TURN ON YOUR INNER MAGNET

One of the best ways to determine how you can put out more positive energy and become magnetic is to notice the body language and actions of people who make you feel good in their presence. If you pay attention, you'll no doubt notice that their body language remains open. They don't cross their arms or their legs. They stand up straight and enter a room with a smile, giving the impression that they're happy to be there. They're good listeners, and they maintain eye contact, showing that they care about the person who's speaking. When they stand with a group, they include everyone through open body language and frequent eye contact. If someone approaches when they're speaking to someone else, they find a way to invite the new person into the conversation. They convey warmth and interest by smiling frequently and gesturing with their hands.

Clearly, the most approachable people in the room are those who appear to be sensitive, non-judgemental, passionate, and compassionate. They make you feel interesting and keep you interested by engaging actively in the conversation. They offer you sincere compliments, and when you mention an accomplishment, they don't hesitate to tell you they're impressed. They often seek out the people who are shy and try to engage them in the activities. They ask questions that evoke positive answers, such as 'What keeps you busy during the day?' They try to determine how they can help each person in the room and operate under the assumption that whatever favours they give will some day return to them.

People with positive energy have a sense of humour. They take the time to remember funny stories that they can tell in social situations. They keep track of what's going on in the world in order to be good conversationalists. They never run out of things to talk about because they lead interesting lives and have great stories to tell. You can cultivate all of these traits. Simply pay attention to humorous stories, read the headlines, and experience life by visiting museums, theatres, and new restaurants.

But what about the people who make you feel negative? If you study the reasons why you feel ill at ease with someone, you will probably discover that they're giving off one or more unconscious signals. These people tend to make little eye contact with others, or their eyes dart around the room rather than focus on the person who's speaking. It may be a sign of shyness, but it comes across as lack of interest. If a man is uptight, for example, he will leave his suit jacket buttoned. Fidgeting and tense body language may be a result of social nervousness, but it gives the impression that the person is bored and distracted. Nervous habits like nail biting and scratching repeatedly will make others uncomfortable.

If you're shy and find it difficult to make eye contact, you simply have to force yourself to look at other people. You will find that you become more comfortable with it as you practise. Try to speak clearly and without hesitation to show that you're confident about what you're saying. If you're easily distracted, practise focusing your attention. This is a common problem since your mind can process words faster than anyone can speak, but allowing your mind to wander is death to confident conversation. Watch documentaries and BBC News, and work at listening to every word. Listening is a skill you can develop, and this practice will train you to maintain your attention in conversation.

Self-consciousness can be a real problem, but the best way to relax is to focus more on the other person than yourself. If they mention something positive about themselves, respond favourably. You might say, 'It sounds like you have invested a lot in your future as a teacher,' or 'You obviously contributed a great deal to the charity's recent success.'

People who lack positive energy fail to show their interest in others. They often interrupt and try to dominate the conversation. They appear distracted and overly anxious to speak rather than listen, sometimes turning their body language away from the person who's speaking. They may even tap one of their feet. This behaviour can convey a sense of superiority, which is often a result of underlying insecurity. These people sometimes 'work the room', quickly moving from one person to another as if to discover the most advantageous person there. In other words, they're out for what they can get, rather than what they can give. Even though it's natural to want to gain something from your new acquaintances, positive energy requires that you focus more on what you can offer others. It will always eventually pay you large dividends.

If you're a passionate person, you may become so excited by the conversation that you inadvertently dominate it. Guard against coming on too strong. You may have no intention of being domineering, but if you push too hard or appear desperate to make your points, you will turn off your listener. Passion is a great way to engage people in what you're saying, but it sometimes needs to be tempered to keep people from feeling that you're trying to force them to your point of view.

If you're unsure of how your energy is perceived by others, *ask*. Friends and associates you trust can let you know where you need to improve. If you try too hard, you will come across as insincere, but friends can tell you if you need to tone down your friendliness. You may even ask a friend to observe you with others to give you an assessment of your energy. If someone appears to react to you negatively, however, don't take it personally. It could easily be a result of their own discomfort, or you may simply resemble someone they dislike.

INJECT POSITIVE ENERGY FOR
RELATIONSHIP SUCCESS

University of Washington emeritus psychology professor Dr John Gottman developed a mathematical formula that can not only tell if a relationship will last, but also when the split will occur if it's doomed to fail. He came up with this formula after observing seven hundred couples over a period of fourteen years. He watches couples closely as they discuss problem topics. The calculus formula is based on an index that measures facial expression, voice tone and speech content, all of which is a characterization of the emotions each person expresses. Positive signals, such as a warmhearted joke or sympathetic nod, get points, but negative signals, such as disdainful eye-rolling or snide comments result in points lost. Specifically, Gottman is looking for such positive signs as interest, validation, affection, humour, and joy, while the negative signs are seen in disgust, contempt, belligerence, domineering, anger, fear, tension, defensiveness, whining, sadness, and stonewalling.

What matters isn't so much what the couples say to each other as how they say it. By keeping track of the positive and negative signals, or codes, a pattern emerged in the happiest and least happy relationships. The happy couples speak almost in one voice because they are so tuned into each other's wants and desires, while unhappy couples not only have no symmetry or respect for one another, but also are so nasty and mean they actually struggle to find positive things to say about one another and their relationship.

If you are familiar with the 'naysayer', he or she is the person who often offers criticism or presents reasons why something won't work. If you have ever been in a relationship with a naysayer (or if you are one), you will know that this kind of negative communication is exhausting for those around this person. Naysayers don't always have negative attitudes; they simply use language that gives the impression of negativity. It is very easy to fall into the negative language pattern, and many of us do so without being aware of it.

An example of a naysayer is someone who tells another person what he or she has done wrong, but doesn't stress the positive things that can be done to remedy the problem, like in the comment below. The information is all there, but it sounds cold and ... negative:

'I am tired of doing everything around the house while you walk in after a day of work and do nothing. You always say you are glad to pitch in then never follow through. Will you please at least help with the kids?'

Contrast this example with a more positive approach:

'I know you have gladly offered to help around the house; what would work best for you? Dividing chores up now or coming up with a plan before we head out each day for work?'

This positive example sounds completely different, though it contains almost identical information. It has a more 'upbeat' and helpful tone.

And another example:

'I cannot possibly allow you to host a party for your graduation since you have neglected to give me any information on the costs involved, the number of attendees, etc. ... Please look into all that along with any additional details and get back to me.'

While this may be polite, it is also exceedingly negative. It includes several negative words—'cannot' and 'neglected', and it has a tone that suggests that the requestor is to blame for the problem.

A more positive approach:

'I am excited about your graduation. I need some additional information about the party you want to host. If you can let me know the expected costs, number of attendees, and any other details that are important to you I will be able to make a decision and get back to you.'

NEGATIVE AND POSITIVE LANGUAGE

Negative phrasing and language often have the following characteristics:

1. Have a subtle tone of blame.
2. Contain words like *can't*, *won't*, *unable to*, that tell the recipient what cannot be done.
3. Do not stress positive actions that would be appropriate, or positive consequences.

Positive phrasing and language have the following qualities:

1. Tell the recipient what can be done.
2. Suggest alternatives and choices available and sound helpful and encouraging.
3. Stress positive actions and positive consequences that can be anticipated.

COMMON NEGATIVE LANGUAGE AND PHRASING

Eliminate common negative phrasing such as the following:

1. Expressions that suggest carelessness:
   a) You neglected to ...

b) You failed to ...

c) You overlooked ...

2. Phrases that suggest the person is lying:

a) You claim that ...

b) You say that ...

3. Expressions that imply that the other person is not too bright:

a) I cannot see how you ...

b) I fail to understand ...

c) I am at a loss to know ...

4. Demanding phrases that imply pressure:

a) You should ...

b) You ought to ...

c) You must ...

d) I have to ask you to ...

e) I must insist ...

5. Phrases that might be interpreted as sarcastic or patronizing:

a) No doubt ...

b) I will thank you to ...

c) I understand, of course ...

d) Let me know as soon as possible ...

POSITIVE PHRASING

A few examples of positive phrasing:

1. If you give me _____ , I can _____ for you.

2. Based on what I hear you saying, it seems you have a different viewpoint on this issue. Let me explain how I feel.

3. Can I suggest that you _____?

4. One option open to you is _____.

5. I can help you to _____ if you can get me _____.

Are You Memorable?

Another way to project positive energy is to make sure you are remembered. Here are three tips for staying in the minds of those you meet:

While you don't want to dress in a flashy way for social functions, you can wear something distinctive. Choose your clothing carefully to stand out subtly rather than merely blend in. You might wear a special tie or a piece of jewellery that could serve as a conversation piece.

Repeat your name, the name of your company, and/or the name of your product when it's appropriate. Think of this information as the 'key words' of your conversation that will help those you meet find you more easily in the 'search engine' of their brains. Be careful, however. Repeating personal information can be a difficult thing to pull off if you lack the proper subtlety. Make sure you use these opportunities wisely. If it's obvious why you're repeating the information, you will appear to be a pushy opportunist, and there is no positive energy in that!

Are You Memorable?

Find a short but interesting story about yourself or your business that will set you apart. Your companions will be much more likely to remember you if they associate you with an unusual story. If you're unsure whether or not your story is entertaining, try it out on a friend or colleague, and only offer the story if it naturally flows in the conversation. Don't interject it out of nowhere.

A PROACTIVE APPROACH TO POSITIVE ENERGY

Never underestimate the power of networking and cultivating positive relationships. Sending out positive energy is about more than simply making a good impression at a business meeting or gathering. You can *create* positive energy by taking active steps. Never miss the opportunity to congratulate someone on their good news or freely share a resource that you think might be of interest (as long as your sharing isn't a daily occurrence that would cause you to appear pushy or intrusive). If you have nothing special to say to someone but want to make contact, you can simply say, 'I really enjoyed meeting you, and I'd like to get together. Could we get together for coffee during the next week or two?' If the other person makes excuses about having no time, you can take that as a 'no' unless you're offered an alternative such as, 'Actually, in three weeks, I would have time.'

Follow up every contact that appears to be remotely advantageous or enjoyable, but don't act like you're best buddies with someone you've just met. Little will turn someone off faster than a person who acts like an old friend when you're merely acquaintances. It comes across as trying too hard, and the other party will absolutely suspect you're trying to get something from them. Instead, *offer* something to the other person—a tip, an article, a contact, or information about an event. Just make sure that you choose carefully. The tip or information should be truly of value to the other person. If not, you will appear as though you're simply trying to ingratiate yourself insincerely.

Introduce people to one another if you think it would be meaningful or helpful to them, or set up meetings where you can act as a host. Connecting people with each other is one of the most effective ways to build relationships, whether you introduce them face to face or by passing along contact information. You will always be appreciated when one of those connections proves to be fruitful.

If you have clients or customers who could benefit from your expertise, consider creating a newsletter with valuable information. Hire a writer to help you compose articles, if necessary, and be careful to make sure the information is truly helpful. Sending newsletters with nothing but a sales pitch or articles that are 'fluff' with no substance will quickly become an annoyance.

Whether or not you create a newsletter, send notes via snail mail to set you apart from the pack. The Royal Mail says that the majority of mail today consists of catalogues and sales letters, so receiving something personal in the mail will definitely be noticed and considered a pleasant extra effort on your part.

Whatever you do, work hard to remember names. A surefire way to destroy a potential relationship is to forget that you've already met someone. Always ask for business cards, and make notes on the cards, including physical descriptions, to help you remember who's who. When you run into someone again, you'll not only be able to say, 'Nice to see you again, Jack,' but you'll also be able to ask, 'So, how are those tennis lessons you were telling me about?' or 'Please tell me about your trip to Fiji!' How special do you feel when someone remembers you in this way and asks you a very specific question that is personal to you? Also consider accepting a business card in the same way those in many Asian cultures do. During a speaking tour in Singapore and Thailand I learned to receive a card face up with both hands, then to take a moment to look at and absorb the information on the card and make a positive comment as well. 'What an interesting logo!' or 'Tell me about the origins of the name of your company,' show sincere interest and send out positive energy.

Using praise is a surefire way to send out positive energy. As every good manager knows, praise must be specific— 'Awesome! Your work with Evan on his presentation skills seems to have helped his confidence during training sessions!' —or it's meaningless.

DO YOU UNDER-SELL OR OVER-SELL YOURSELF?

Only a lucky few actually enjoy self-promotion. Not only are we taught as children not to brag, but there are so many opportunities to be shot down by someone else that it's a very vulnerable thing to praise yourself. Despite the discomfort, your success in social and business situations is largely dependent on your ability to make confident talk about yourself. Finding the right balance can be difficult, however. If you under-sell your strengths and abilities, you may come up short. If you over-sell yourself, you will either come across as arrogant or compensating for insecurity.

If you want to avoid under-selling yourself, ask friends and associates to enumerate your strengths and talents. This will help you to feel you have the proper perspective, and it will get past your own judgements and insecurities about your performance. You may even learn some new great things about yourself! If you find it extremely uncomfortable to discuss your talents, you can always attribute the information to your colleagues. You might say, 'My colleagues tell me that I'm diligent and detail oriented', or, 'My partner tells me that I have a real empathy for animals ...'

Determine your best qualities. Perhaps sensitivity, wit, compassion, humour—then project them to the world. Before meeting new people or attending important events, focus on strength rather than your insecurities. Success will result if you do the following:

- Meet as many people as you can.

- Learn to be sociable.

- Smile at people naturally.

- Be kind, considerate, and generous to all the people you meet.

- Listen and be open minded.

- Learn to like yourself.

- Change the things you don't like about yourself.

- Study what makes people popular and copy their methods.

- Try to be happy and content with who you are as a person.

- Remove negative aspects and influences in your life permanently.

Making friends and dating often requires promoting yourself. Promotion may seem like a 'dirty' word but under close examination promoting yourself for a new opportunity in your personal life is not much different from doing the same in your professional life.

At work the best way to prevent over-selling yourself is to talk about a specific project. Discuss the challenges you overcame and how you did it. Then, be sure to mention the benefits of your actions to the company. If you worked with a team, praise their performance as well as your own. Be careful not to take full credit for something unless you truly accomplished it without help. Say only what's necessary to make the pertinent points about the project. If you go on and on, you will appear to be trying too hard, and this will convey underlying insecurity.

Here is an example of specifically illustrating your accomplishments in the workplace: 'I spent two years opening fifteen distribution centres in several Asian and European countries. It was very rewarding and demanding work, which gave me a crash course in accounting, corporate valuation, business strategy formation, and implementation. It was also a crash course in dealing with different cultures and personalities. There were problems along the way, as employees were reluctant to accept the changes I was asked to implement, but I found that if I truly listened to their concerns, I was able to offer solutions and help them to stay calm about the changes. As a result, my company now has fifteen successful new centres across the globe, and all of them are still bringing in substantial revenue for the company.'

The Interviewee: The Energy Advantage Gets the Job

In order to have a successful interview, you simply must become comfortable with selling yourself, but under-selling or over-selling in this situation are the fastest ways to get fired before you even get hired! Follow the advice in other chapters about preparing your answers and watching your body language, but it's even more important to follow the advice in this chapter about projecting positive energy. If your energy is negative, too shy, or too domineering, you may as well stay at home. Don't worry, though, it only requires a bit of work to fine-tune your interview presentation. If you take the time to do the work and discover where you need to improve—videotaping yourself or asking friends and associates for their honest opinions— you have an excellent chance of landing that dream job.

Remember, however, that just because someone conducts interviews for a company doesn't mean they're good at it and have positive energy themselves. No matter what you receive back from the interviewer—closed arms, fidgeting, or distracted eyes—keep your energy and body language positive. This is a time when you *don't* want to mirror the body language of the other person. You may be surprised that the interviewer suddenly becomes more comfortable and begins to mimic *your* body language.

The Interviewer: The Energy Advantage Gets the Best Candidates to Want the Job

Interviewers often forget that they are *also* being interviewed by applicants. You're representing your entire company to each candidate who walks through the door, and if your energy is negative, you'll lose the best people for the job. Try not to ask rote questions like, 'What's your biggest weakness?' or 'What would you like to be doing in five years?' Ask questions that are specific to each applicant. All it takes is a quick review of the CV before the interview to come up with questions that will help the candidate feel at ease. Listen intently to the answers you receive, and never take phone calls during an interview unless they're urgent.

While it may seem advantageous to have a superior attitude that puts candidates off balance, it will cause the most talented people to look elsewhere. The bottom line is that a company will flourish if it can attract the finest people in the field.

At a networking event when someone asks: 'How have you been?' or 'How's work?' make the most of the opportunity to share upbeat news. So many times we fall in a rut by responding to 'How have you been?' with 'busy' or 'same old, same old'. Instead, be prepared to offer a more stimulating response that never borders on bragging: 'I have been very well. We had the opportunity to bid on some exciting new business recently,' or 'I travelled to Chicago for an interesting meeting last week.' Two things occur when you supply these embellished responses. First, you did not fall into a rut of conversation clichés, and secondly, you gave your contact something to talk about with you, thus preventing an awkward moment filled with silence. Please avoid those 'elevator speeches'. I too have heard that a good networker gives a pitch about their business, service, product, or career search when asked 'How are things?' The lack of sincerity is usually evident. We have all heard these self-serving pitches, and I know I am sick of them. Please do not tell me more than I need to know. Just give me a sentence in response and the potential for connecting is planted.

STAYING IN THE MOOD

When it comes to positive energy, make sure it's genuine. People will notice if you're trying too hard or pouring it on too thick. So, what do you do when you're going through a rough time and have no positive energy to spare? You don't want to pretend to be positive, which will probably only make you feel and appear more tense, but you can learn how to alter your internal mood! There are numerous ways to accomplish this, and you can experiment until you find the ways that work best for you.

For example, keep a list of some of the happiest moments of your life. Whenever you need to be 'on' to meet a client or attend a meeting or event, you can help yourself to feel more positive by recalling these moments. If you're *really* feeling down, take the time to recall your happy moments in as much detail as you can. You might recall a special vacation, your wedding day, the birth of your child, or the day you won an award. Remember sights, sounds, smells, tastes, and feelings. Fellow professional speaker and past president of the US National Speakers Association, Scott Friedman, is known for concealing five dollar bills wherever he goes. In books, under pillows, left behind on an aeroplane seat for the cleaning staff to find, knowing that he has planted a future smile on someone's face. Or Scott will surprise and endear himself to his dining companions when he uses his special fork that stretches four feet across a table and removes a carrot from someone's plate. Another US professional speaker and trainer Tim Gard recommends a packet of 'Big Bucks' (a large amount of money) to the managers and supervisors he works with. If you are the manager, supervisor, or decision maker who always hears, 'You should do it, that's why you get the BIG BUCKS!' now you have a tool to counter those remarks. Pass them out so everyone has the big bucks! That is a way to dispel negativity in the workplace.

As I enter a venue for a meeting, a luncheon or networking event, or a presentation, I plant a 'real' smile on my face and check my posture for comfort and confidence. This ensures that I present myself in a fresh and positive way and leave my worries behind as I enter the door. A smile in any direction almost always guarantees a smile in return.

Another way to alter your internal energy is to play music that you love. You might respond best to music that makes you want to dance, or you may prefer soothing classical music. If music fails to move you, try watching a DVD of your favourite comedy act. Laughter can alter your mood faster than almost anything.

You can only learn how to switch your energy organically from negative to positive through trial and error. Everyone is different. Think of yourself as a method actor. You're not pretending; you're manipulating your psyche like a musical instrument to project the best possible energy. If you do that, the energy will be true, not false. If all else fails, focus on making your companions feel good. You might just find yourself feeling better as a result!

9

BUILD CONVERSATIONAL CLOUT

Recognize how to influence others and achieve your goals using specific conversational techniques.

You already know the importance of the energy you project, but what about the words you use? If you use passive language, you will sound hesitant and unsure. If, on the other hand, you use aggressive words, you will come across as overbearing and pushy. Neither of these types of language does anything to improve your confident conversation. Luckily, there's a third type of language that is neither aggressive nor passive. It is *assertive*.

Words that are assertive project confidence and knowledge without forcing yourself on someone else. In the last chapter, I described the most approachable people in a room as those who are attentive and sensitive to others. This doesn't mean that you have to be touchy-feely and wishy-washy, however. Assertive language is straightforward and direct without undermining yourself or anyone else. It's neutral in a way that conveys honesty and openness.

WHAT DO YOU MEAN BY THAT?

Which type of language do you use in different situations? If you aren't sure, you may be sending messages that are different from your intentions. Listen to yourself and others, and think about how the use of certain words can lead confident conversations astray. In the interest of politeness, people often hold back what they really want to say, which causes them to appear uncertain or meek. Directness doesn't mean you must forgo being polite. If your words are too vague, however, you're barely communicating at all. Assertiveness is the happy medium.

- **Vague questions and statements.** When you fail to let someone know exactly what you want or need, you set yourself up for disappointment. Don't ask your friend: 'When can I have that loan repaid?' Instead, ask: 'Can you have the loan I made you repaid by the end of the month?' Don't say: 'We need to talk about what you plan on doing once you graduate as soon as possible.' Instead, say: 'Can you let me know some good times this weekend when we can discuss your post-graduation plans?'

- **The 'if' questions.** We use the word 'if' when we feel tentative. The problem is that it sets up a low expectation and makes you appear uncertain. Don't say: 'If I could take a moment of your time ...' Instead, say: 'Could I have a moment of your time?' Don't say: 'If I can get the information for you ...'

This sounds like you're unsure of yourself. Instead, say: 'I'll check this out and let you know what I find out.'

- **Qualifying statements.** It's easy to forget that downplaying your knowledge can make you seem overly cautious. Don't say: 'I was going to say that the tone you use when you talk to me sounds disapproving.' Instead, say: 'The tone of your voice sounds disapproving.' Don't say: 'I believe it may be necessary to purchase a new car this year ...' Instead, say: 'In my opinion, we will need to purchase a new car this year.' Allow yourself to assert your beliefs and opinions without apology.

- **Silly questions.** Stop to think about some of the questions we ask regularly that make no sense. Don't ask: 'Can I ask you a question?' You have already asked a question before getting permission to ask your question. Instead, say: 'I'm sorry to interrupt, but I'd like to talk to Jennifer about our plans for next week. What time are you available?' Don't ask: 'Can you spell your name?' Of course, this person can spell his or her name! Instead, say: 'Please spell your name.' Don't ask: 'May I ask if you've seen the latest Harry Potter film?' Instead, ask: 'Have you seen the latest Harry Potter film?'

- **Obvious statements.** Sometimes, you may try to be emphatic but end up inadvertently putting yourself down. Don't say: 'To be honest, I would rather eat at home than face all that traffic.' Does this mean you are sometimes *dis*honest? Simply say: 'I would rather eat at home than face all that traffic.'

- **Judgemental statements.** Keep your statements factual. Don't say: 'Your recipe did not make sense,' which is insulting and accusatory. Instead, say: 'The recipe was hard for me to understand. Please walk me through it.'

- **Demeaning statements.** Watch for subtle statements in which you put yourself down. If you say, 'I only help with the food after services,' you are undermining your contribution to the function. Instead, say: 'Making contributions is not an area I know anything about, but I can put you in touch with Barbara, who handles the finances here.' In an effort to get out of completing a task, you may find yourself downplaying your role: 'I'm just her mum; I don't know anything about cars.' Instead, say: 'Cars are not something I know a great deal about. Let's talk to a mechanic.'

- **They made me do it.** It is not uncommon to use 'have to' in a sentence, but it conveys an obligation, either on your part or on the part of someone else. When you say, 'I'll have to check with my girlfriend/boyfriend,' you imply that you are controlled by your partner. Instead, say: 'I'll check with my girlfriend/boyfriend to see if that time is convenient.' When you tell someone else that they 'have to' do something, it sounds as though you are trying to be the one in control. Don't say: 'You'll have to come by later because I can't spare a moment right now.' Instead, say: 'I can make myself available to talk with you about that tomorrow. What time would be best for you?'

- **I-statements.** While you want to have give and take in any conversation and ask questions about the other person, assertive language involves I-statements. In this way, you take responsibility for what you think, feel, and do. You are not passing blame onto someone else or pretending that you know less than you do. I-statements help you to deflect blame while still being assertive. For example, if you say: 'When you don't pick up the tickets on time, you cause all sorts of problems,' you will likely be greeted with defensiveness. Instead, say: 'I'm unable to deliver the tickets to the other kids when they do not arrive to me on time. I need them by no later than 3:00 p.m. on Friday of each week.' This is assertive, and it shows how the other person's behaviour is affecting you.

Take the time to think about what your words are truly communicating. Some colloquialisms in the English language do not serve you in confident conversation. Consider how to 'flog' something is to sell it. It also means to beat something with a whip, but when your wife tells you she flogged the old TV it is more likely that she has sold it than beaten it (I hope!). There are underlying meanings that we tend to forget, but they have a subconscious effect on others in conversation. Speak from a place of strength, and your confident conversation will be much more successful.

Assertive Body Language

When someone is assertive, they make eye contact with you, which is an indication of sincerity. They mirror your body language, and they gesture when it is appropriate. An assertive person will stand straight and solid on both feet, facing the other person directly. An assertive vocal tone is level, calm, and moderate, conveying confidence in what is being said, while a raised or high voice indicates uncertainty or deception.

TECHNIQUES FOR ASSERTIVE CONVERSATION

There are numerous ways you can steer a conversation back to the matter at hand, even when the other party is trying to dissuade you from your goal. These techniques allow you to be assertive without becoming aggressive or defensive, and they often prevent you from entering into an argument.

- **Partial agreement.** When someone says something critical, you have an opportunity to deflect the negativity by agreeing with them *in part.* For example, your child may say: 'Don't you think you've made nap time too long?' Don't say: 'I don't think it's too long, and besides, if I don't make certain that you get the rest you need you won't be ready for the recital this evening.' This is a needlessly defensive response, and there is no reason to explain yourself. Neutralize the comment with a partial agreement: 'You're right. That was an extra long nap time.'

- **No apologies.** Another way to handle critical remarks is to accept your responsibility without apologizing. It disarms the person who is criticizing you, leaving them with little fuel to throw on the fire, as you offer empathy for their point of view. A partner might say: 'You never have time for the family.' You can respond by saying: 'You're right. I haven't always had time to spend with the family.'

- **Compromise.** When it makes sense to do so, compromise. In the situation above, it may be to your benefit to offer your partner an opportunity to set up a regular time to spend with the family. You could say, 'You're right. I haven't always had time the time to spend with the family because of my work schedule. Can we set up times during that week that work with my schedule?' Only consider a compromise, however, if you can maintain your self-respect in the process.

- **Calculated repetition.** In both business and personal conversations, some people will try to manipulate you into an argument or may simply ignore your statements to push their own agenda. A technique to respond to this involves repeating your original point in a calm voice no matter what the other person says.

  Let's say your cable company contends that you never returned your cable box and expects you to pay £150 for it. Here is a way to utilize the repetition technique:

  You: 'I have a receipt showing that the technician took it with him, and I won't be paying for a box that I clearly returned.'

Customer service representative: 'We have no record of the return, so you owe the £150.'

You: 'I have a receipt showing that the technician took it with him, and I won't be paying for a box that I clearly returned.'

Customer service representative: 'If you don't pay the £150, your service will be cut off.'

You: 'I have a receipt showing that the technician took it with him, and I won't be paying for a box that I clearly returned.'

If you still fail to receive satisfaction, get the name of the head of customer service, and waste no time straightening out the situation with the person in charge.

You can also use this technique in a conversation power play by starting your repetition with 'I just said …' If someone continues to push, you can push back by acknowledging their statement, followed by a repetition of your point. For example, you might say: 'I hear that you want me to give you more time to paint the house, but the work needs to be finished by 1 June.' If this doesn't work, you can say: 'I have told you several times that the work must be finished by 1 June, but you seem to be ignoring me.' In order to deflect an argument, you might offer assistance: 'I'm sorry that you feel there isn't enough time to finish the work on schedule, so let's discuss what needs to happen in order to get it done by the deadline.'

- **Take a breather.** If emotions run high, the most assertive way to handle the situation is to stop before an argument ensues. You can simply say, 'If we take some time to cool off, we'll be able to have a more productive discussion.' If the other party refuses to let it go, you can say: 'We'll discuss this later when emotions aren't running so high.' Then, simply leave.

- **Interrupt an interruption.** When someone interrupts or does something distracting, you can bring the attention back to the subject at hand by stopping and directly addressing the problem. In this instance, it is best to use an I-statement to avoid creating an argument. For example, you might say: 'I need to bring us back to talking about getting your school work completed and handed in on time. I become frustrated when the discussion digresses in a direction that won't accomplish our goals.'

- **Interrupt an argument.** Sometimes, a conversation gets out of hand before you know it. When this happens, you can interrupt the trajectory of the argument by simply saying, 'Let's take a break. What happened to cause us to argue?' Humour can be helpful in a situation like this, if it is appropriate: 'I must have had one too many cups of coffee today!' See if you can get to the core of the issue and come to a compromise between you. For example, you might say: 'Let me see if I understand your point of view. Are you trying to say that …?' or 'I know that it's difficult to get your school work done with so many after-school activities that are important to you, so let's take a breather and set up a time to talk about this later today.'

If you find that the other person continues the argument despite your best efforts, you can be more assertive: 'It's unproductive for us to argue about this. We become defensive and get nowhere. Please get back to me, letting me know which activities are the most important to you and how you can maintain your school work at the same time. I will then do my best to come help you work this out so we are both satisfied.'

The combination of assertiveness, body language, positive energy, and sensitivity to others will give you a finesse that few possess. It may sound complicated, but it just takes some thought and practice. You'll find that your efforts are well worth it, giving you the edge in all situations—business and personal.

10

GET CLOSURE

Uncover satisfactory ways to end a conversation and leave a great final impression.

Nothing ruins a great movie like a lousy ending. You might have enjoyed every moment, but if the conclusion leaves you cold or confused, you walk away disappointed. The same is true of confident conversation. A great first impression can be cancelled out by a conversation that ends poorly. People may remember the energy they felt the moment you first met, but it is the last thing you say or do that they will remember most vividly.

Everyone has experienced conversations that stop abruptly or end with a whimper. Have you ever told a story, only to have someone walk away abruptly without a proper goodbye? It leaves you wondering if you were boring. Have you ever been stuck in a conversation with neither of you knowing how to move on? There are specific conversational techniques you can use to end a conversation on a high note and leave your companions wanting more.

EXIT STRATEGIES

The best way to handle the closing of a conversation is to be prepared. If you have any social anxieties, be ready with several appropriate phrases for use in high stress situations. First and foremost, be friendly and sincere. Whether you need to end your talk for a specific reason or simply want to circulate around the room, look the person in the eye and shake hands, if appropriate.

If you need to take your leave when someone has finished telling a story, be sure to have a legitimate excuse for walking away, and try to show appreciation for their story. You could say, 'I need to catch my train, your work on your yard is very impressive!' If you truly want to connect with this person again, be direct: 'Thanks so much for your helpful tips. Could we get together for a few minutes sometime next week? I'd love to call you and set something up if your schedule allows.' Or, 'Can we exchange phone numbers? I would like to be in touch.' You can also use the opportunity to end the conversation with a promise, such as: 'I'll email you that article tomorrow, and I look forward to hearing your thoughts about it.'

There are several techniques you can use in different situations to close a conversation and move on. Watch for cues from your companions that they are ready to move on. They may not know how to close the conversation, but if you see their eyes wandering around the room or a period of silence falls between you, simply say, 'Well, it was very nice to meet you, and I hope we can chat again.' Another clue that your companion may be ready to move on is repeated answers such as 'um hmm', which indicate a lack of interest. Whatever you do, be careful not to become one of those people who go on and on despite these cues. If you genuinely want to continue the conversation, ask if you can schedule a time to talk later.

After you have spent time at a social event or a meeting, try to revisit as many people as you can to say goodbye and let them know how much you enjoyed meeting them. Refer to the person by name, and say something short and sweet: 'Thank you again, Sam, for the information about the computer repairs. I'll let you know how it turns out,' or, 'It was a pleasure to meet you, Sarah, and I look forward to seeing you at next month's meeting.'

CONVERSATIONS THAT WON'T DIE

We've all experienced it—the conversation with someone who just can't or won't get to the point. The best way to handle this situation is to try to clarify what the person needs from you. You might ask, 'So, would you like me to help you by contacting the head of the committee?' or simply, 'How can I help you fix this?' You can quickly end the conversation by saying, 'I'll look into this and get back to you as soon as possible,' or, 'I can touch base with the chair of the committee and email you today with answers to your questions.' If the party is angry, you can try summarizing the problem as a way of creating calm: 'I under-stand you expected the committee to make the budget requests this morning and that without it done your schedule has been turned upside down. I will do my best to get it done this afternoon.' Often, people just need to feel that they've been heard. If you're not the right person to handle the problem, quickly refer the overzealous conversationalist to the correct individual: 'I'll be glad to put you in touch with our budget committee chair.'

If you're in a social situation, you can introduce the person to someone else and ask the two of them to excuse you as you graciously take your leave. If an introduction isn't possible, however, simply say, 'I need to visit some other attendees before lunch is served, I really enjoyed meeting you.' Another possible comment is: 'There are several people here tonight I haven't seen in a long time, and I want to say hello. Would you excuse me?' If a person is very clingy or a chatterbox, you might be able to placate her or him by asking if they would like to join you as you are heading to the buffet table for a refill. The buffet table, bar, or art display is a good place to engage others and not be held hostage by one individual.

Some people speak so fast that they barely take a breath. Don't feel obligated to explain why you need to end the conversation, but look for a tactful moment to interrupt. You can interject a comment such as: 'Yes, I know exactly what you mean. Unfortunately, I need to go now. Maybe we can revisit this at a later date?' Be sure to leave the conversation in a courteous manner. This person could know someone important to you. The longer you allow your time to be infringed, however, the more frustrated you will become, running the risk of letting your aggravation show. Never forget that your time is just as valuable as anyone else's.

You may also find yourself in conversations with people who offer you much more personal information than you ever wanted to know. Find an opportune moment to interject and say, 'I'm really sorry to hear about that. I hope everything works out for you.' If this happens repeatedly, stop asking, 'How are you?' Simply say, 'Hello, Tony. Good to see you.' Of course, you can also simply apologize for having to cut the conversation short and say you need to visit your sister across the room. Don't allow yourself to be caught in a lie or hurting people's feelings, however. If you say you need to chat with your sister, go drop by your sister's table rather than catching up with someone else.

DATING DIGNITY

Here's a classic scenario. Imagine you are having a glass of wine for your first face-to-face date. The conversation hasn't been flowing so easily and your brain is working overtime thinking of excuses why you don't want to see him or her again. Whether he or she asks to see you again before leaving the table or as you walk to the car, the anticipation of how you'll respond is mounting. What's a nice person to do?

Below, you'll find a list of ways to say 'no, thank you' with kindness and grace. Preparing a few key phrases in advance will help you to feel more confident about your ability to escape unwanted situations. Practise the lines that work best for you and feel the most comfortable. Here are a selection of kind ways to say 'no' to a request for a second date (or first!):

- This was nice, but the chemistry I'm looking for isn't quite there.

- I enjoyed our time together, but the spark just isn't there for me.

- I enjoyed meeting you, but I don't feel that certain something I'm looking for.

- Thanks so much, but I don't think we're looking for the same thing.

- This has been fun, but we have very different ways of looking at the world.

- I enjoyed talking to you, but we don't share enough of the same interests.

- Thanks for the coffee, but I don't think we share the same outlook on life.

- I had a nice time, but I'm looking for something more serious.

- It was nice talking to you, but I don't think it's in the stars for us.

- I appreciate the offer, but no thanks.

HAPPY ENDINGS

Certain situations require that you end your conversation with a bang. You need to make a great *last* impression to match your great *first* impression. Here are some specific ideas to use in various circumstances.

- **Landing a date.** Asking someone for a date is very important. That is your real first impression. Make your conversation for asking very casual. If you want to get started by asking for his or her phone number, do so in a friendly, non-threatening way. For example, instead of saying, 'So, can I have your number?' try something like, 'I'd really like to stay in touch. Is there a number where I can reach you?' Don't use those worn-out lines like, 'Would you like to go with me?' It's too open ended and can lead to awkward follow-up conversation. Do not ask, 'What are you doing Friday night?' It's again too open. It may leave your potential date wondering exactly what you have in mind. The other person doesn't know if you're just curious about what she/he is doing on Friday night or if you want to do something with them ... This opener is one that is a comfortable fit for most: 'I would really like to get together and do something with you sometime.' Now, she or he can't say, 'Sorry, I'm not free,' because you haven't set the time or place yet. In fact, you have not even asked for a date yet! Now is your chance to observe his or her reaction. If it's negative, no need to continue and you have not even been rejected! But if he or she responds with a smile and says 'OK', continue with: 'I would really like to go out with you when you're free, how about a drink at Blacksmith's on Thursday?' First, she/he can't just say, 'Sorry, I'm not free,' since she has already said that she would like to go out with you. If she/he really is not free that day, simply ask her/him when a good time will be. Secondly, she/he has to be free sometime, right? If you are uncertain or uncomfortable about getting together—go with a group. Ask the question: 'There's a bunch of us going bowling on Saturday, would you like to go?'

- **Job interviews.** Don't forget the importance of a memorable ending to your job interview. You want to leave the interviewer with an excellent feeling about you. Use the moment to reiterate your enthusiasm and your most important points. Keep it short and sweet, but dynamic. You might say, 'Thank you so much, Ms. Bennett. I'm very excited about the prospect of working for XYZ, and I believe I could bring some innovative ideas to the company. I enjoyed meeting you, and I look forward to hearing from you about the position.'

What Should I Say, or Ask, as I'm Leaving a Job Interview?

The question to be asked that will help guide you the most is: 'Can you please share with me how the rest of the selection process will go?' This is what I call a 'sitting-down' question, not a 'standing-in-the-hall' question. It may take a few moments for the decision maker you are talking with to be able to give you a good answer.

The answer should include these elements:

- Approximately *how far* the company is in the process. Extremes are 'You're the first person we've talked to,' and 'We've met a dozen candidates already.'
- Approximately *how many* more times you'll be expected to come back for interviews.
- *Key people* in the selection decision that you have yet to meet.
- Approximate *timing* for the remainder of the process.

If the response is, 'We're very early in the process,' that should be taken into account as you consider other opportunities.

- **Trade fairs.** You may find yourself in a situation where you are manning a booth at an industry expo or trade show. In this situation, you need to make contact with as many people as possible, which may require you to close some conversations quickly and skilfully. If someone strikes up a conversation during a slow time, you may have the luxury of holding a lengthy discussion. If there are lots of people visiting your booth, however, you will need to move on. You can simply say, 'I'd love to talk with you about this more, but I need to attend to the other visitors here. Can we set up an appointment to discuss this in detail?' If you don't wish to set up an appointment, you can offer marketing materials and ask the person to call you with any questions.

If there are no other visitors at your booth, but you wish to end the conversation, you might say, 'Mr Foster, it was great meeting you, and I look forward to discussing how we can work together. I don't want to keep you because I know there are many other booths for you to visit. Thanks for stopping by, and enjoy the conference.' If this doesn't work, you could try, 'Please take a look at our website, and get back to me with your thoughts,' or, 'Let me give you our free sample. Take it with you, share it with others, and let me know what you think.'

• **Meetings.** You will gain a reputation as a great leader if you close meetings well. You don't need fanfare, but letting a meeting fizzle out without a proper closing does nothing to keep people motivated. When a meeting comes to an end, first ask if the person taking the minutes has all the information he or she needs. Next, thank everyone for their participation and make a positive statement about what was accomplished in the meeting. You might say, 'This was a very productive meeting. I want to thank everyone for your contribution. We have some exciting plans, and I look forward to working on these projects with all of you.'

- **Presentations and speeches.** The end of a presentation is almost as important as the beginning. There's nothing wrong with summarizing your points, but if you say, 'I will now summarize my main points for you,' your audience will immediately tune you out. They assume they've already heard it and no longer need to listen to you. You might use a visual aid, such as a picture or PowerPoint slide to make your final point. Another technique is to choose a statement, quote, story, or question that illuminates your central theme. It should be dramatic enough that it will stay with your audience long after you've left the podium. Make it something they'll think about—perhaps a call to action or a challenge of some kind. For example, if you're giving a motivational speech about getting more sales, you could end your presentation with: 'How will you challenge yourself to make more sales this month? How many more will you book—ten, twenty, thirty? If you try the techniques I've outlined today, I'll bet you book at least ten more. Will you join me in taking that bet?'

IF YOU DON'T ASK, YOU DON'T GET

You simply cannot wait for your customers to tell you they're ready to buy. If you do, you'll probably be waiting forever. When you want to close a sale, you need to ask for it. If the possibility of rejection gives you chills, there is no alternative but to get over it. Rejection is an inevitable part of life, especially in business, and even more so in sales. Think of most rejections as nothing more than a 'not yet' answer. It may be that you simply haven't established enough trust with your customer. Work toward creating goodwill and integrity in your relationship, and you will move from the 'not yet' answer to a definitive 'yes'.

How do you know when to ask for the sale? Every situation is different, so knowing when to ask for business is often a matter of intuition. If you use all of your confident conversation skills, observing your prospect's body language, verbal cues, and energy cues, you will determine the right time. You won't always receive an immediate 'yes', of course, but you *will* discover what information your prospect needs in order to get to that 'yes'.

The most obvious time to ask for the sale is after you have outlined the benefits of your product or service. It should be built in to your sales presentation, but make sure that you have tailored these benefits to the needs of each customer. What problem does your product solve for this particular prospect? How is it better than the other products on the market, and how is it cost effective for your customer? If the customer appears to be convinced that your product is a viable solution, now is the time to ask for the sale. Anticipate potential objections and be ready to counter them. If your prospect does come up with a viable new objection, however, don't lie about your product. If necessary, tell your prospect that you will check on it and get back to them as soon as possible. This kind of integrity will go a long way toward eventually getting you that sale.

When you ask for the sale, your prospect may not be quite ready to sign on the dotted line, but it may be time to ask for a commitment to move on to the next step. You could ask, 'Can I speak with someone on your team next week about our product?' or, 'Would you like to explore this further?' Be careful not to ask questions that make you sound as though you've lost patience with your customer. Don't say, 'What will it take to convince you our product is the best one on the market?' You can, however, ask the customer to outline his or her reservations: 'Can you tell me what concerns you have about working with our company?' or ask one of my favourites: 'What will it take to get your business?'

Ask and Ye Shall Receive

Here are some ways to ask for the sale:

'It looks like our product is exactly what you need to solve your software issues. I would really enjoy working with you to implement it in your organization. How about we get the paperwork going?'

'Why don't I get you started with this today?'

'I can work out the details with you right now if it's convenient. Shall we get started?'

'If I've answered all of your questions and concerns, can we move forward?'

'I think it would be fun to work on this together. Do we have a deal?'

Whenever possible, make like the Godfather, and make your customers an offer they can't refuse. You may not always be able to do this, but offering a trial or sample of your product or a money-back guarantee is a great way to gain trust. You can say, 'Why don't you use our product for two weeks risk-free? I'm confident you'll agree that it's the best on the market.'

Sometimes, a customer has a problem making decisions. You might hear a general question like, 'Why should we choose your company over your competitors?' You could try to answer with a litany of your company's attributes, but you may have no way of knowing if your comments are valid to the customer. In fact, some of your company's attributes may not be advantageous for this customer at all. Turning the question back to the customer can help you to clarify the information they need to say yes to the sale. For example, you could say, 'I'd be happy to tell you why you should choose my company, but I haven't even asked you about your needs yet. If you tell me the problems you have, I can tell you whether my company can solve them for you.'

The most important thing to remember when it comes to asking for the sale is to *keep asking.* Don't be relentless about it, but as you continue to develop trust with your prospect, periodically ask for business. And never be afraid to use humour. When I was struggling to get my speaking business going, I would often send an old running shoe or trainer with a note enclosed asking, 'I've got one foot in the door, what will it take to get in the other?'

You have more chances to make mistakes in the middle of a conversation than you do at the beginning and at the end. Closing a sale, a meeting, a speech, or a conversation is a lot like the ending of a date. If the goodnight kiss goes sour, you may never get another date with this person. Great closings require finesse and skill, and that's what confident conversation is all about.

PART 2

APPLYING CONFIDENT CONVERSATION SKILLS

11

SEE YOUR OWN REFLECTION

Come to see yourself through other people's eyes, thus enabling you to build stronger relationships with customers, business partners, co-workers and colleagues, managers, employees, friends, and family members.

You have worked on projecting positive energy, you've perfected your body language skills, and you have practised confident conversation in a variety of situations. Yet, you may still find that you're not always making the connections you would like. Perhaps an important relationship dissolved or is disintegrating, a job or sale eluded you, or you may have found that a recent networking attempt fell flat. So, what more can you do to increase the odds of having fruitful confident conversation?

You can further fine-tune your skills by seeing yourself through the eyes of others. Finding out what others think can sometimes be as easy as asking for direct feedback. When that isn't possible, observe body language and verbal cues to get an idea of how you're coming across. No matter what your method of finding out how others see you, the more objectively you can evaluate your confident conversation abilities, the better you will be able to improve your skills and build beneficial relationships.

When you step outside your ego and analyse your performance from the perspective of someone else, you can better see your weaknesses and work to step up your game. You might even picture yourself communicating with someone before an actual conversation takes place. Imagine that you're another person meeting you for the first time. As objectively as possible, what would your impressions be?

Pay attention to when you receive positive results and when something appears to be amiss. What confident conversation techniques have you used in each of these instances? Begin to keep track of your communications; thinking back on what appeared to work and what appeared to fail. You might take notes after each encounter to see if there is a pattern that emerges. If so, you'll have a good idea of what you need to improve. For example, if your child repeatedly misunderstands responsibilities you describe, you probably need to work on becoming clearer. Don't take every situation to heart, however. Sometimes, you simply will not 'click' with someone, and it has nothing to do with your confident conversation skills.

Feedback need be nothing more than repeating a message that was heard, for example, 'So what you are saying is that you expect me to have my whole room spotless before I can head out to the game?' Responsive feedback can lead to clarification, understanding and solutions. Failing to give feedback can lead to misunderstandings and sometimes to bad feelings and frustration, 'What I said is I expected you to spend time getting your room tidied up before heading for the game.' Giving a *closed response to feedback* indicates that a person either has not heard or understood, or chooses to ignore the other person's remarks, 'That's fine!', 'Whatever you say!' In other words, it cuts off communication.

An *open response to feedback* indicates that you have heard the person and you are interested in what they have to say; 'Tell me more,' and 'I see what you mean,' lets the speaker know that you really want to hear what he or she has to say. Non-verbal sources of feedback often speak louder than the spoken word. Consider the teen that comes in late from a date. The expression on the parent's face will probably prepare him or her for the unpleasant reception that follows—even before the first word is ever spoken. Another technique when giving feedback is the use of 'I' messages. An 'I' message can help you relate what you are feeling to another person without blaming the person for the problem. There are three steps to constructing 'I' messages:

1. State the behaviour: 'When ...'
2. State your feelings: 'I feel ...'
3. State the consequences of the behaviour: 'Because ...'

Consider the example of a mother who is continually arguing with her daughter over helping out with the laundry. Instead of saying, 'You make me mad when you don't help with the laundry!' the mother might try saying, 'When I have to do all of the laundry by myself I feel frustrated because I don't have any time left to spend with you.' The mother gets her point across without directly blaming the situation on her daughter. Using, 'when ...', 'I feel ...', and 'because ...' statements will help family members as well as friends learn to offer feedback and more importantly communicate more effectively.

Imagine this scenario. Your partner is trying something new with great enthusiasm. It may be a new way to hang wallpaper, prepare a new recipe, or singing lessons. The project or effort does not meet your expectation. What is your reaction? How do you give your feedback? Feedback must be constructive. Criticism—instead of appreciation of the positive aspects of the work—for instance belittling, finding minute flaws, negative feedback, will potentially kill any interest he or she had. Responding positively to someone's progress or efforts generates goodwill. Negative feedback can create a feeling of discontent in the mind of the recipient. He/she may develop hostility toward their partner, parent, or friend. In a family or with a friend it is expected that we be supportive. For instance, if a glass is knocked off the table and makes a mess, we can react in two ways. One, we can laugh at the mess, and second, we can say something about how reckless and messy the person is. The second approach will not help your relationship. Always remember that you are there to be supportive, even of each other's mistakes. It is important to be a positive guide to your partner, your child, your friend, so that they feel a trust with you. That is the essence of a successful and happy relationship.

Questions like: 'How am I doing, Honey?' often make us uncomfortable. These questions are difficult to ask, because we may think we aren't doing well and don't want to call attention to that fact. Or, we may be doing just fine, but don't want our special someone to think we expect or are soliciting a compliment. We also may feel that we are revealing too much of ourselves, risking an unfavourable response. In the end, we would rather assume that no news is good news.

MISCONCEPTIONS ABOUT FEEDBACK

Here are some misconceptions about feedback that might help dispel the fear and help build better relationships:

1. Feedback is a 'grade' or a 'judgement'. Not necessarily. Feedback is simply information. Imagine that someone told you that they won't be at your party next week. That is strictly informational feedback. Would it be accurate to say that they aren't coming because they think your parties are awful? Would it be accurate to say that your parties are so great that people hate to miss them? Neither would be accurate. If you really care, you might ask for more information or do an objective assessment of your parties and ask yourself how you feel about attending!

   Asking 'why' is, of course, the riskier course. But it is also the one that will give you more information about this particular person and give you an opportunity to give this person more information about yourself. That is how relationships are built.

2. Not only is feedback a judgement, it is a negative judgement. As youngsters, particularly in school, many of us grew up being told what was wrong rather than what was right. And some of us learned to identify that feedback with ourselves as people, rather than with our (changeable) behaviours.

   So, even now, we have difficulty thinking about the possible validity of a suggestion that we do something a different way, because we can't get over feeling that we are being criticized. So, let the person you are dealing with know that you would like some positive information about how you are doing, too.

3. 'No news is good news.' Lots of us think that if we aren't getting feedback at all, everything is just fine, particularly when our partner is involved. Most partners regard giving feedback as very difficult, and yours is probably no exception.

   One reason for only negative feedback from your partner may be that he or she thinks you know your strengths better than you know your weaknesses. Or, he or she may be assuming that because you are not asking for feedback, you don't really need it. Whatever the reason, don't settle for 'no news is good news'—it doesn't promote building relationships.

   What to do? Routinely enlist your partner's appraisal of how things are going, in a general sense and in specific areas that may have been touchy spots or sources of conflict.

Are You as Clear as Crystal?

If you notice squinting eyes or tilted heads when you speak, you may be having trouble getting your points across. If your communications are unclear, people will have difficulty giving you constructive feedback. Strive for better clarity in both your spoken and written confident conversation with these tips:

- Be as concise as possible. While it may feel natural to say more in an effort to be understood, less is more when it comes to clarity. The more you say, the more you may muddy the waters. If written communication, go over your instructions several times, reading them as if you're someone learning the information for the first time. Continue to revise until you say no more or no less than necessary.
- Don't pile several thoughts or instructions into one sentence. Keep each point in its own sentence. If your sentences are short, they will be clearer.
- Visualize your instructions being completed in order to include all of the steps. Think about directions that you find with a toy or a piece of furniture that you must put together. They're almost inevitably unclear, aren't they? If the person writing the directions stopped to visualize someone putting the item together, they might be less likely to leave out important steps.
- When you offer directions to someone, speak slowly, and watch for verbal cues that you were clear. Don't be

Are You as Clear as Crystal?

condescending and talk down to someone, but do clarify
that you have been understood. If it makes sense to do
so, ask the person to outline the main points in order to
verify your instructions.

- Use words that are specific, not vague. Pronouns such
  as 'he' or 'she', 'they' and 'them' can confuse your
  listener. Avoid words that fail to pinpoint a certain time,
  such as 'soon' and 'sometime'. Instead of saying, 'We'll
  check with them about it soon,' say: 'I will check with
  George on Friday about the reception schedule.'

MANAGING THOSE PESKY EMOTIONS

Seeing your own reflection has a great deal to do with self-awareness. The more you understand your own unconscious motives and reactions, the better you will be able to evaluate your performance and make necessary adjustments. If you operate on emotional auto-pilot, you will find it much more difficult to maintain positive relationships professionally or personally. Integrity is practically impossible if you know little about your underlying emotions.

Everyone has emotional triggers—those hot buttons we discussed earlier—that activate something painful from the past. These triggers can send you into a tailspin of irrational behaviour that is detrimental to your objectives. If a new experience feels remotely similar to something that caused you pain in the past, you may leap to assumptions that the new experience is going to cause you the same pain. Your defence mechanisms will then be activated, which will affect your behaviour unless you catch yourself before the behaviour becomes destructive. When emotions become heightened, take the time to stop before you react. This will allow the adrenalin rush to subside. If you wait before communicating, you will be able to dissipate the trigger.

The more you're able to put yourself in someone else's shoes, the more you will be able to see yourself through the eyes of others. Perceiving situations from another's perspective will allow you to be empathetic to the feelings of colleagues, employees, and customers. Empathy is the most powerful thing you can develop in order to maintain harmonious relationships. Even when you must fire someone, you can do so in a way that acknowledges the employee's dignity and worth.

Here are some questions that may help you to uncover hidden motivations and emotional triggers:

- When someone criticizes you, how do you feel? Do you become angry with the person who is critical, or do you turn your anger inward? Do you plummet into self-defeating thoughts about your worth as a person?

- Do you frequently pass judgement on your friends or members of your family? Judgements are usually a result of fear and a reflection of self-judgements. If you see someone with a weakness that you fear you possess, it may activate a fear response. You will maintain better relationships with others if you understand they're doing their best. If you're in a position to offer criticism put your judgements aside and offer it gently and constructively. Try to help others improve. Again, empathy will help you reduce the habit of judging others.

- Do you judge the people you dislike more harshly than you judge your friends? Pay attention to determine if you dismiss behaviours in your friends that you criticize in others. Work hard to avoid hypocrisy, maintaining the same criteria for everyone. If you're known for your fairness, you will cultivate trust from many in your life.

- When you make a mistake, do you find yourself wanting to deflect blame? The best way to deal with a mistake is to accept it, apologize, and try to rectify it. No one likes to deal with a mistake, but integrity requires that you take the high road and take responsibility for your actions. In the long run, this will be much more beneficial to you, as you will establish yourself as a trustworthy and honest person.

- Do you spend a lot of time complaining about your partner, your team mates, your job, your coworkers, or your friends? Frequent complaints create negative energy for yourself as well as others. Everyone avoids negative people. Even your friends who tend to be negative will step away from you when they aren't in the mood to commiserate. People who complain and judge are rarely trusted, as everyone will wonder what you're saying behind their backs.

• Do you ever notice that you dislike someone right away? If you stop to evaluate why, you may discover that it is due to an emotional trigger rather than something the person said or did. Others may judge you harshly for the same reasons, and while it's human to do so, it's also unfair. Perhaps someone reminds you of a person you dislike, or they use a phrase that holds unpleasant memories for you. Stop to evaluate why you dislike someone, and make an effort to give people a chance rather than pass quick judgements.

• Your judgements are often the result of beliefs that you may have carried throughout your life. Others will also carry beliefs that may cause them to judge you without giving you a chance. For example, if you're in sales, you might run across a customer who simply doesn't trust any salespeople. The customer automatically assumes you're lying simply because you're a salesperson. While the customer may have had a bad experience with someone else, this belief certainly doesn't apply to all salespeople. You may also carry false beliefs about yourself. For example, if an art teacher harshly criticized your efforts, you may falsely believe you have no creative talent. Do you carry any of these beliefs that get in the way of your judgement? To gain a true perspective, ask trusted friends to give you a reality check about your beliefs.

Some Personal Prejudices

- Corporate executives cannot be trusted.

- I'm not as important as my supervisor.

- If I'm not in control, nothing will go right.

- I'm never valued for my work.

- If I don't do what everyone wants, I'll lose my job.

- If I ask for anything, I will be disliked.

- My opinion isn't valid.

- Wealthy people are selfish and superficial.

- Corporations don't care about their employees.

- Employees will try to get away with doing as little work as possible.

Once you have become aware of some of your bad habits, how can you become less of a slave to your emotional triggers and begin to create new habits? *Positive self-talk.* Research has shown that you can dissipate negativity by talking yourself out of it. When you catch yourself judging someone or complaining, *stop.* If you make a commitment to pay attention to your behaviour, you will begin to catch yourself. If the emotional trigger is very strong and seductive, you may need to sit quietly and talk to yourself about choosing a new and more productive path. If a criticism sends you into a tirade against yourself, remind yourself of your accomplishments and the things you have done for others. Recall compliments and accolades that you have received which will counteract your self-criticism. Remember that one criticism doesn't negate everything else you have achieved in your life.

FEEDBACK ANYTIME?

Soliciting feedback from close friends and family, employees, customers, and even colleagues is the easiest and most direct way to find out how you're perceived. But timing plays a role in asking for opinions. For example, if you are coming out of a breakup you may want to gain your own perspective on the causes before soliciting opinions from people who interacted with the two of you during your time together. Without taking the time to sort out your own truths about the breakup it will be easy to be influenced by others who most certainly did not witness the relationship from the inside as you did. Or if you have just launched a new product, website, or marketing campaign, you need to give it some time before you ask for feedback. People need to have a chance to form an opinion before you ask for it. Otherwise, you will get useless feedback, as people will answer your questions without enough information.

Ask for feedback in positive terms. Never say: 'I fear my overall discipline with my child has not been consistent. Can you tell me what I did wrong?' You will have planted a seed in the other person's mind that your parenting is poor, even if it isn't. Instead, say: 'I would really appreciate your feedback on my discipline style. I'm eager to hear both strong and weak points so that I can work to improve my parenting.' This statement allows the recipient the possibility of saying, 'I found no inconsistencies with your discipline style at all. I think your discipline style is just fine.'

When receiving feedback, remain quiet and listen carefully until the other person is finished. Then, you can ask questions to clarify their points. Be careful to avoid defending your position, even if you feel the criticism is unfounded. If you become defensive, you will gain a reputation as someone who can't handle feedback. Thank people for their feedback, and if you can use it, let them know how you will use it.

GIVING AND ASKING FOR FEEDBACK

Giving feedback is the act of verbally telling the other person how his or her actions affected you. Being open to receiving feedback means you are curious about and willing to hear how your actions affect other people. Most people don't get very much valid feedback in their daily lives, and they long for it.

When are some of the best times to ask for feedback?

- **After a job interview where you did not get hired.** Some interviewers will refuse to answer your questions, but if you make it clear that you understand you weren't chosen and simply want to improve your interviewing skills, many interviewers will be impressed by your desire to grow.

- **After a speech or presentation.** Use detailed forms to ask your audience for feedback. If few people seem to be willing to complete the forms, offer some incentive, such as a free CD, book, or report, in exchange for the feedback. No matter how experienced you become as a speaker, there is always room for improvement.

- **When you're considering a project** and want to determine if there is sufficient interest within your organization.

- **After you have completed a project.** If your supervisor fails to be forthcoming with praise after you have completed a report or project, don't hesitate to ask how you did. Be ready to receive constructive criticism, but take this information with the enthusiasm of someone who genuinely wants to learn. If you worked with a team on a project, ask each member to give you feedback on your performance. You can ask specific questions if you want to ensure that the feedback is constructive.

- **During your annual or semi-annual review.** Study past reviews, and have an open discussion with your manager about your strengths and weaknesses. Ask for assistance in maximizing your performance. Your superiors will be impressed with your eagerness to develop your skills and talents. Sometimes, your reviews are simply delivered to you in writing. If this is the case, schedule a meeting with your supervisor to discuss the feedback in detail. Taking the initiative in this way will not only offer you valuable information, but your interest will set you apart from your coworkers.

Getting to Know Your Customers

Customer feedback is absolutely essential in order to maintain the customers you have, learn how to gain new ones, and increase your bottom line. Create surveys online or in some other form to find out what your customers are thinking about your products and services. This will help you to determine where you need to make adjustments.

Getting to Know Your Customers

Surveys are time consuming for your customers, so offer them some sort of incentive for completing the survey, such as a discount or free item.

What sorts of questions should you ask your customers? Here are some examples:

XYZ Company responds right away to my needs and concerns:

Strongly agree
Somewhat agree
Don't know
Somewhat disagree
Strongly disagree

I purchase XYZ Company's products for the reasons below:

Value for money
Quality
Customer service
Product features

How satisfied are you with the service provided by XYZ Company?

Very satisfied
Somewhat satisfied

Getting to Know Your Customers

Don't know

Somewhat dissatisfied

Very dissatisfied

What is your overall impression of XYZ Company?

Very positive

Somewhat positive

Don't know

Somewhat negative

Very negative

What information would you like to receive from XYZ
Company?

New products and services

Specials and discounts

Trends in the industry

Tips for best utilizing our products

Efficiency tips for running your business

Industry statistics

Competitor news

If you could change anything about XYZ Company's
products, what would it be?

What changes to XYZ Company's service would make you
more satisfied?

THE OTHER SIDE OF THE FEEDBACK FENCE

When you're the one offering feedback, you have the opportunity to flex your empathy muscles. Catherine the Great once said, 'Praise loudly; blame softly'. The more positive feedback you are able to give initially, the smoother negative comments will go down. Focus on strategies for improvement rather than criticism. Do everything you can to avoid eliciting defensiveness. If the person receiving your comments does begin to defend, defuse the situation as quickly as possible by offering encouragement. You might say, 'Please don't feel the need to defend yourself. Everyone has areas where they can improve their performance, and these are simply places where you can become even better at what you do. We simply want you to reach your full potential for your own fulfilment as well as your success here at XYZ Company.'

Unless you must offer unsolicited feedback, wait until someone asks for your opinion. Giving your opinion to a colleague or even an employee when it isn't necessary will breed bad will. If someone makes a mistake that must be addressed, offer feedback immediately. Be specific and positive in your feedback. Don't say: 'Your report was prepared in the wrong way.' Instead, say: 'The opening of your report was excellent, and I have some ideas how you can make future reports even better. Let's set up a time to bounce some ideas off each other.' Don't make someone feel that he or she is 'always' wrong. Don't say: 'You never remember to check with Paula regarding your weekly schedule.' Instead, say: 'I've noticed that you've forgotten three times to check with Paula regarding your weekly schedule. Perhaps if you make a note to remind yourself each week, you will solve the problem.'

Resist the urge to avert your eyes from your subject. Making eye contact will help the recipient of your feedback to feel more comfortable, and it will help you to convey warmth as you dole out your constructive criticism. Practise mirroring body language when appropriate, and shake hands at the end of the meeting in order to show your goodwill. If your subject appears to be worried about the feedback, offer additional encouragement. You could say, 'Don't worry about your review, Bob. If you apply yourself, you'll be able to improve by next time.'

Seeing yourself through other people's eyes is a skill that requires sensitivity. As you develop your ability to be empathetic, coupled with reading the energy and body language of others, you will begin to see the nuances and underlying motives in both yourself and your partner. You will recognize emotional triggers that get in your way, and you will see some of these same triggers reflected in the behaviour of your colleagues, employees, and clients. As a result, your understanding of human psychology will increase, and you will be able to handle all sorts of confident conversation situations on your feet with finesse, compassion, and the appropriate amount of assertiveness.

12

UP THE ANTE

Identify ways to go that extra mile in order to ask for—and get— recognition, praise and acknowledgement, referrals, a raise, a promotion, or a commitment.

George Bernard Shaw is famous for saying: 'The problem with communication is the illusion that it has been accomplished.'

Is the courtesy of acknowledgement too much to ask? Asking for acknowledgement of an act of friendship, an energetic approach, or a wonderful calming influence? Not exactly the same as the emails arriving, many from unknown senders, *demanding* acknowledgement of receipt or 'Notify Sender'? Asking for acknowledgement of an email may be asking for too much, but how about asking for some mention about the positive difference you make in his or her life? How important do you think daily acknowledgement and emotional support, curiosity, and encouragement are to receive from your partner, your parent, or even a friend?

Everyone needs to be praised and recognized for who they

are and what they do. Everyone needs to know that the time and effort they spend is making a difference and that they are making a contribution that is recognized. If you rely solely on your partner's initiative to show you appreciation, you may get less than you want and almost certainly less than you need to not feel taken for granted. Fortunately, no one needs to feel they are a victim when it comes to praise. If you want more praise, following are some strategies you can use to get it.

MODEL THE BEHAVIOUR

For individuals who complain about their partner who never praises or acknowledges them I wonder, 'When was the last time they did the same for their partner?' One way to subtly influence the behaviour of another is to treat that person as you'd like them to treat you. You might, for example, say to your partner, 'Mark, thanks for taking time to tell Janice what a great organizer you think I am—it really made my day!' A typical partner might respond with, 'Oh, I didn't realize that was so important to you,' and then—human nature being what it is—almost inevitably be a little more on the watch for similar instances to acknowledge you. Teach your child at a young age: 'Sarah, it made me feel great when you mentioned to your brother how much fun you have on our family vacations. Knowing that you appreciate our holidays makes me want to plan as many as we possibly can.'

ASK FOR THE PRAISE

Many people feel awkward in asking for praise. They feel that they shouldn't have to ask and that asking for praise will diminish its value. I disagree on both accounts. You can bring up the topic in a general way such as by saying, 'Mary, I've never told you, but it really means a lot to me when you make comments about my reading with the kids. Hearing you say that makes me feel good, and also makes me sure to keep it up even when I am tired.' After all, no one is a mind reader, and getting praise makes it easier to focus future efforts better. 'Jake, your appreciation for the help I gave you with the move meant a lot to me. It is easy to help a friend when the help is acknowledged.'

How do you keep from seeming like you are being egotistical or simply currying favour? Be honest and direct and emphasize the positive and practical aspects of receiving immediate and specific praise and acknowledgement. As the saying goes, 'Recognition is the breakfast of champions.' Don't be afraid to seek an adequate serving.

In many relationships we feel taken for granted, that family or friends *assume* that things will be done and never acknowledge or show appreciation. If you are feeling used or taken advantage of, it is time to sit down and have a long talk. A relationship should be a way to grow and promote both individuals, not for one individual to take advantage of the other.

Asking for a raise or a promotion is enough to make anyone work up a sweat. Receiving a 'no' is bad enough, but you might worry that simply asking could jeopardize your job. It may feel like a precarious position, but you need to make sure you get your just rewards. If you sit back without receiving the recognition you deserve, you will begin to resent your employer and lose passion for your job. That is certainly no way to live. Worse yet, you may wait until your resentment causes you to ask for a raise in an angry frame of mind. And *that* is certainly no way to reach your objective.

So, what can you do to increase the odds of getting the raise, promotion, or recognition you desire without risking the goodwill you have worked so hard to establish? You can cultivate certain confident conversation skills to help you negotiate with your boss and strengthen your position. As you proceed don't forget our discussion of timing in Chapter 7. Think about your supervisor's schedule, as well as your company's schedule, when deciding the best time to ask for a raise or promotion. Think as carefully about *when* you ask as *how* you ask.

NO SUCH THING AS EASY MONEY

When you want to ask for a raise, begin to think about your role within the company from the perspective of your superiors. Your value to them is based on how much you have improved the company's bottom line. In short, what have you done for them lately? You may feel entitled to more money based solely on the fact that you've done your job well, but your employer is unlikely to see it that way. You have to go that extra mile in order to stand out and earn your salary increase. It may seem unfair, but in the majority of cases, this is the reality of today's business world. If you want to make confident conversation, you need to have something *big* to talk about.

Finding a way to shine and increase your value is the best way to ensure that you receive your raise or promotion. If you develop a reputation as a team player who is always willing to help, you will almost certainly be among the first in line for accolades. This may require some time and planning, but it will be time profitably spent. Don't think of it as giving your employer something for nothing. Think of it as an investment in your future. Don't take on responsibility without letting your supervisor know you're doing it, however. You may need approval to begin or join in a project. Plus, if your superiors aren't aware of your extra efforts, your accomplishments might go unnoticed.

So, what can you do to become more valuable within your company? The first thing to do is simply *request more responsibility*. Ask your immediate manager for a meeting. Here are some examples of ways you can approach the subject:

'I would like to meet with you to discuss my future development and what more I can do to contribute to the team. When would be a convenient time for us to talk?'

'What can I do to make your job easier?'

'Please give me assignments beyond my current level. I welcome the challenge and feel confident in my abilities.'

During your meeting, tell your manager that you would like more opportunities to prove yourself. This will be a subtle alert that you're not only interested in doing a good deed, but want to move up in the company, financially and otherwise. If you want to be more straightforward about your intentions, simply say: 'I would like to move up in the company. What would you advise I do to merit a raise or promotion?' or, 'I feel like I'm doing excellent work, but I understand that my salary is less than the market in our area. What can I do to earn an increase within the next year?'

Ask if there are any projects that you could join, or if you could launch a new project of your own. If your manager has difficulty thinking of anything for you to do, ask that you be considered as soon as something becomes available, but don't rest on that request. If you do, you may be resting forever. Sometimes, you have to take the initiative and look for your own opportunities to show your worth. Talk to colleagues about their projects, and look for ways that you could become involved. Better yet, look for beneficial projects that no one has considered, and speak to your superiors about launching it on your own or with your own team.

Ways to Become an Extra Mile Runner

- Prepare a report that shows how efficiency could be improved, which translates to time or money saved. Include a cover sheet with your name on it to make sure there is no question you are the one who has created the report.
- Always give yourself extra time to complete work, promising to deliver it later than you expect to be able to

Ways to Become an Extra Mile Runner

finish it. This gives you the opportunity to turn it in early. Make it as attractive and professional as possible, and find a way to do more than you were asked to do.

- Look for new business, if appropriate, and network to find referrals for the company.
- Try to learn a skill that will be highly valued in the organization—something that few, if any, other employees can do.
- Learn personal things about clients in order to set you apart in their eyes. You might learn about their children, acknowledge a birthday, or find out about their vacations and favourite restaurants. Make reference to this personal information when you talk with clients, being careful not to become *too* intrusive or personal. When customers bring up your name to your boss, you place yourself at the front of the line for a promotion, raise, or bonus—perhaps without even asking for it. When customers bring up your name to referral sources, you potentially gain more business.
- Be proactive, and come through in a crisis. If the company can depend on you, there will be no reason to turn you down for a raise or promotion.
- If you make a mistake, have the integrity to come clean about it. This will pay more dividends for you in the long run than trying to hide it or pass the blame on to someone else.
- No matter how much you do for your company's bottom

Ways to Become an Extra Mile Runner

line, if you complain or have difficulty getting along with people, you will undermine your efforts. Remember that your attitude is more important than your skills, because skills can be more easily taught than attitudes.

- Think of yourself as a freelancer or a vendor who must constantly prove themself worthy to be hired again. Better yet, do your job as if you own the business, taking pride in all you do.

When you take on new responsibilities, try to find tasks that can be easily quantified in monetary terms. Search for projects that will give you high rewards for your efforts. In order for your new responsibilities to merit a raise, you need to be able to show that your work has improved the company's profits. If you're asked to do a task that you feel will be less than advantageous for you, ask if you can have an even more challenging assignment. This will potentially allow you to dodge a no-win task without sounding as though you simply don't want to do it.

GATHER YOUR AMMUNITION

When the time comes to request that raise, promotion, or bonus, request a meeting with your supervisor to discuss your role in the company. Say that you'd like your supervisor's advice, and strive to make the meeting as easy as possible for him or her. Don't say, 'I want more money,' or, 'I need an increase because of additional expenses.' This is not a good reason for your company to give you a raise. Again, look at it from the point of view of your superiors. A raise is due only if you have done something to merit it. Talk about what you have given or what you can offer the company rather than what the company can offer you. Discuss the situation as if you were an objective observer rather than someone emotionally caught up in the outcome.

Maintain a diary that keeps an account of what you have done each day or week for the company. This will help you to remain professional and confident in the meeting. Prepare spreadsheets, if possible, that show your efforts in concrete pounds and pence. You may also write down a few stories of your successes, as well as client and vendor testimonials. (Ask for these testimonials, as long as you don't feel it will undermine your company's relationship with the vendors or customers.)

Sit down with your diary, and write a list of bullet points regarding all you have done for the company, and have it ready to present during your meeting. Only include accomplishments within the last couple of years, add testimonials, and be armed with your stories. When you present the list to your boss, say something like: 'I really enjoy my position at XYZ Company, and I'm looking forward to learning more and contributing as much as I can. I've taken the liberty of preparing a list of my most recent accomplishments, and I believe these will show that a salary increase is in order. I would appreciate it if you would take some time to review the list and let me know if you agree.' Exude confidence that you will absolutely receive the raise, but stay friendly and warm so as not to appear arrogant. And don't expect an immediate answer. Your boss will have to take some time to review your list, and your increase may very well need to be discussed by a committee or approved by someone higher in the organization.

Do as much homework as you can to determine what kind of increase you can expect or request. What was the percentage of the last increases given in your organization? Conduct research to find out the salaries of similar jobs in your part of the world. Check advertisements online, in newspapers, and in trade publications, but be careful not to expect city salaries in more rural areas, for example. This will never fly. If your salary is lower than others in your area, you can argue for an increase based on the information you find. Take inflation rates into account as well, but remember that an increase for inflation is not an increase for performance. If everyone receives a raise for inflation, you should receive an additional increase for your extra efforts on the job. Don't forget to add the benefits and perks you receive from your employer, including pension plans, training, etc. These are all at additional cost to the company.

Never threaten to leave the company if you don't receive a raise or promotion. This will undermine any efforts to get what you want. If you do choose to resign in an effort to get a salary increase, don't count on it. You may or may not receive an offer

---

When Making Your List, Ask Yourself These Questions About Your Performance:

- Have you reduced costs?
- Have you increased sales or profits?
- Have you brought in new customers or saved relationships with current customers? (This may actually merit a bonus.)
- Have you improved efficiency?
- Have you solved company problems?
- Have you trained others?
- Have you saved time that has, in turn, saved money?
- What have you done since your last salary increase?
- What have you done or what do you do regularly that is beyond your job description?
- Do you put in extra hours?
- Have you received training or learned a new skill that adds value to your job?

---

from your employer, and if you don't have another job waiting in the wings, you're out of luck.

Remember that every company operates within a budget, and raises are hardly a priority. This doesn't mean that a company doesn't value its employees, but no CEO wants employees to get the impression that obtaining a salary increase is easy. Some companies claim to maintain a freeze on salaries, but this may not actually be the case. If your raise is denied due to budget considerations, find out if you can obtain a commitment for an increase in a certain period of time. If you are asked to take on additional responsibilities, you can ask to be considered for a raise or bonus after a few months. Just make sure that any such agreements are in writing.

If your employer is simply unwilling to allow you to take on more responsibility in order to move up within the company either in terms of position or salary, it may be time to look for a new employer. Only you can decide if you want to stay in a situation that will keep you at the same level without hope of advancement.

YOU MAY NEVER HAVE TO SELL AGAIN

Whether you are an employee of a corporation or a business owner, referrals are the key to increasing the bottom line. Working with you must be memorable and unusual in some way in order to get referrals. Think more in terms of service to your customers than selling products to them, and if you don't know what your customers consider great service, ask! Receiving customer feedback is the best way to improve your offerings. Build long-term relationships as you do friendships, and always follow through with what you say you will do. Again, it's all about going that extra mile. If you are endlessly 'referable', you may never have to make another cold call.

As soon as a customer compliments you, it's the perfect time to ask for a referral. You can say, 'I'm so pleased that you're happy with our service. Do you know anyone else who might benefit from what our company has to offer?'

You can also receive referrals from other businesses, turning them into 'referral partners'. Return the favour, of course, and actively try to do so as quickly as possible after you receive your favour. Learn about your referral partners' businesses so that you know how to find the right referrals for them. If necessary, ask for materials that explain their business. Seek out partners who will be in a position to help you network with advantageous people and high-quality customers.

Don't keep tabs on what you're receiving in return from your referral partners, however. Simply assume that your favours will come back to you, either directly from the person who has received the favour or from someone else.

Always thank your referral sources. Letting them know you appreciate their help will only get you more referrals and enhance your relationship with your current customer. You can even host dinners or events to show appreciation to your best customers, asking them to bring a friend.

Asking for a raise, a promotion, or a referral can be a nerve-wracking proposition. As difficult as rejection can be, concerns about maintaining your relationship with your boss, your customer, or your company can prevent you from asking for what you deserve. If you seek ways to stand out from the crowd and make yourself indispensable, you will not only have more confidence when asking for what you want, but you will vastly increase your odds of receiving great rewards.

I 3

DEAL WITH STAGE FRIGHT

*Draw upon your confident conversation skills in order to overcome
your presentation fears.*

Mark Twain said, 'There are two types of speakers. Those that are nervous and those that are liars.' If you suffer from stage fright, you're in excellent company. Most famous speakers, broadcast journalists, actors, and musicians experience performance anxiety every time they find themselves in front of an audience. After all, speaking in front of an audience may be the *most* confident type of conversation.

The good news is that audiences can rarely see your nerves. They can't tell that your heart is beating hard in your chest, and they can't see the butterflies in your stomach. What's more, they want you to succeed because they fear public performance as much as you do, and they admire you for stepping up to the podium.

Our previous chapters about body language and positive energy can help you a great deal when dealing with stage fright.

Armed with these confident conversation skills, you will automatically feel more at ease because you will know specific ways to present yourself as confident and upbeat. There are additional skills you can cultivate as well to combat the fears that can make even the best of speakers quake. As a professional speaker who has delivered close to one thousand programmes I have learned a lot about overcoming stage fright. I remember the first time I spoke in front of a group. There I stood in front of 100 other potential instructors who wished to teach at Colorado Free University, a life-long learning institute in Denver, Colorado, USA. Each of us had to stand up and introduce ourselves and our proposed topic to the group. This was in 1992 and I can capture the moment like it was yesterday. My heart beat so hard it seemed to overpower the words coming out of my mouth. My voice shook and I rushed through my words. As I took my seat, I knew I was a flop and had no chance of being selected. Fourteen years later I am an internationally recognized professional speaker with over one thousand presentations under my belt. But it took me years to overcome the stage fright. And I still work on my craft as a professional speaker all the time.

Fear of public speaking is simply your *perception* of a situation that is in the future. Giving a speech is not a life-threatening experience, but if you perceive that you might fail or be ridiculed, your mind will perceive it as a threatening experience. The more afraid you become, the more out of control you feel, and this only compounds your anxiety. If you're able to change your perception of public speaking, you can eliminate the fear. It may be easier said than done, but it's possible! If nothing else, you will learn to manage your fearful responses and reduce your anxiety to a minimum.

Be Prepared!

The single best way to prevent stage fright from getting the better of you is to be so prepared that you know the short congratulatory speech for your parents' fiftieth wedding anniversary or your presentation to the town council backwards and forwards. Practise to such a degree that you could speak extemporaneously without flinching. You can memorize whatever you plan on delivering, but never recite it word for word. Your presentation should be conversational and not rigidly polished. You should know your subject or goal so well that you can waver from your written words without falling off course. If you are faced with a speech, *do* memorize your first couple of lines, however, so that you can recite them in order to give yourself a jump start. This will help you get past those first few moments of stage fright.

Practise in front of the mirror, in front of friends, or on videotape, if necessary, to feel more at ease. Try to make your practice sessions fun so that you begin to associate speaking in front of people with something enjoyable. If possible, join Toastmasters or obtain the services of a speech coach. Nothing will do more for your confidence than a bit of coaching.

The first thing to recognize is that stage fright is a natural survival mechanism which causes a release of adrenalin and cortisol. These chemicals are stimulants that cause your heart rate to increase and your body temperature to rise. If you needed to run in response to a threat, your body would be ready to take off. Blood leaves your stomach, which is what sometimes causes 'butterflies' or nausea.

When you're very excited about something, you experience many of the same physical responses, so what you experience as stage fright can easily be thought of as enthusiasm. Again, it's all a matter of your perception. Some speakers worry if adrenalin *isn't* pumping because they're concerned they aren't generating enough energy to keep the audience engaged. Think of your heightened body responses as the process of getting your engine running and ready to take the audience by storm.

Top Tips for Making a Toast

Need to make a memorable toast? The following are a few tips that will help you with your next toast.

1. **Do your homework.** A toast for a buddy at a stag night is very different from toasting him at the wedding reception. Take the time to learn about your audience. Who are they? What will they find touching, meaningful, or funny so that you can craft a toast appropriate for the event.

   Ask about the length of the toast. Toasts are generally around two minutes.

Top Tips for Making a Toast

2. **Craft a suitable toast.** Match the tone of your toast to the event. Jokes may be well-received at a casual meal with friends, but not at a solemn dinner. Always remember what you want your desired effect to be. Use your own words and speak from the heart. It will be more meaningful. Keep your toast brief. The focus should be on the honoree, not you. Be complimentary. The point of a toast is to say something nice. Exclude inside jokes unless you are willing to spend time setting up the joke for everyone.

3. **Practise, practise, practise.** Practise your toast several times. Aim to repeat your toast without notes. Go to the venue and practise your toast, on the day of the event Make certain to speak to different members of the audience before your toast. You can focus on these individuals when you speak.

4. **Gain everyone's attention.** Obviously, clicking glasses to get your audience's attention works. This is a sure fire way to break fine crystal so consider standing up and using eye contact to quiet your audience and get their attention.

5. **Hold yourself confidently.** Stand up, especially for large parties and dinner parties of six and more people. Keep your body open (i.e., no crossed arms; feet just less than shoulder-width apart). Hold a glass of wine, champagne, or a liquid that looks like wine or champagne in one hand.

Top Tips for Making a Toast

6. **Make eye contact.** Look at the honoree while you deliver your toast. Also look across the audience, making eye contact with a few people throughout the crowd. This gives the appearance of addressing the entire crowd.

7. **Speak slowly and deliberately.** Take a breath to calm your nerves and make sure everyone is looking at you before you begin. Speak very slowly so that everyone can understand you. If needed, use short silences to calm your nerves in the middle of your toast.

8. **Sip, not chug, from your glass.** Lift your glass and ask everyone to join you in toasting the honoree, at the end of your toast.

STAND UP TO YOUR FEARS

There are numerous ways you can combat stage fright. Some of them help to relax your body, while others focus on the psychological issues that stand in your way. In other words, stage fright is truly 'all in your head', but it manifests itself physically. If you alter your body's responses, you might be able to calm your mind, and if you change your mind's perception, you might be able to relax your body automatically. Try several of these techniques to determine which ones work best for you.

- **Self-talk.** One of the easiest ways to work yourself into a frenzy before a presentation is to 'what if' yourself to death. 'What if I forget what I want to say?', 'What if someone asks me a question that I can't answer?', 'What if they laugh at me?' Everyone has these fears, but you can counteract them by giving yourself positive 'what ifs'. For example, 'What if they're impressed with my knowledge?', 'What if I make my daughter proud with my toast at her wedding?', 'What if I actually enjoy imparting information to my audience?', 'What if I speak to the group as if they're all old friends?'

- **The worst-case scenario.** If your mind is filled with all of the things that can go wrong, dissipate these fears by imagining the worst possible outcomes. Follow your negative 'what ifs' to their conclusion. If everyone were to laugh at you, what would you do? Would you laugh with them and make a self-deprecating joke? If you stumble on your words, you could say, 'Oops! Looks like I forgot to untie my tongue this morning!' If you imagine how you would handle the worst-case scenarios, you will probably relax with the knowledge that you could survive. And the best news is that all of your worst fears are highly unlikely ever to happen.

- **Eliminate unknowns.** The more you know about your audience, the organization, and the venue, the less afraid you will be. Who will you be speaking to? What do they want to learn from you? Is the room large or small? Will you be on a stage? Will there be a podium? Will you be using a microphone? Make sure you know the answers to all of these questions. Visit the venue ahead of time if at all possible, and double-check with the organization to ensure that they truly understand your topic. If you're speaking about marketing techniques, your presentation will be different from if your audience is a group of advertising executives, as opposed to a group of home-based business owners.

- **Visualize.** Spend a great deal of time picturing yourself giving the perfect presentation. Visualize yourself projecting confidence and warmth, answering questions intelligently, and interacting with the audience. Picture the audience responding to you favourably. The more you imagine a successful outcome, the more relaxed you will become. In fact, when you finally give your presentation for real, it will feel as though you have already done it.

- **Make it about your audience.** When you're nervous, one of the best ways to calm yourself is to put your focus elsewhere. Direct your attention outward and away from yourself. Concentrate on what your audience needs from you, and strive to give it to them.

- **Create a happy atmosphere.** When fear has you by the throat, think happy thoughts. This may sound Pollyanna-ish, but it works. Keep a list of the best moments of your life. Include your successes in business, as well as happy personal moments. Review this list whenever stage fright takes hold. You can also call a friend for a pep talk, listen to music that calms you, or watch a favourite comedy film or stand-up routine. Laughter will relax both your mind and body. You may have other hobbies that will calm you prior to giving a presentation, such as gardening, building model aeroplanes, painting, or singing.

- **Stay in the moment.** Don't let distractions get the better of you. If you make a mistake, gloss right past it or make a joke about it. Then, move on. If you dwell on mistakes, you will feel even more nervous ... Keep in mind, the audience does not know what to expect from you and is not familiar with what you plan on saying. They do not know if you have missed a line, or forgotten to include a piece of information. Prepared speakers know that although we know what mistakes we made, our audience is clueless. If you see people in the audience whispering or yawning, don't become rattled.

- **Make contact before your speech.** Arrive early if at all possible and chat with audience members. If you make friendly contact with just a few people, you will feel much more at ease, and you will make a great first impression. The inside information or personal asides you gain can be worked into your presentation and will win the hearts of your audience. Smile at everyone, even if you don't feel like smiling. Eventually, your smile will become natural as others smile back at you, and your stage fright will begin to dissolve.

How to Make a Public Comment

Are you a parent who wants to make a comment at a school meeting? Maybe you are a resident speaking up at a Neighbourhood Watch meeting. A citizen who would like your voice heard at a council meeting? Speaking up is a great way to show that you care about something and to get your thoughts across to the public, a representative or group of representatives along with persons in authority.

How to Make a Public Comment

Gather any facts you may want to be presenting to them.
Write down your comments or speech. Though people
who read straight from a paper sometimes sound like
robots and have trouble making eye contact, they still get
their point(s) across better than those people who don't
plan at all and stumble all over their words or meander off
point. If you are comfortable with and have the ability to
rephrase a few lines here and there while presenting, it
will help make it sound more human. Sit through the
meeting until you are called up or called upon. You will feel
relaxed and confident throughout the meeting, but when
you know you will be up soon, you'll have that feeling
where your heart and stomach are quivering. That is
completely normal, especially for first-timers. Go up to the
podium or microphone, or simply stand up confidently
when called. If appropriate, thank whichever person
called you, then introduce yourself, state why you are in
attendance and why you feel personal about it. Make your
comment. Before taking leave thank those you directed
your comments towards or the audience at large.

TAKE CARE OF YOUR BODY

Even if you manage the anxiety of your mind, you may find your
body still has the muscle tension, dry mouth, and/or butterflies.
You might be tempted to take a chemical of some kind to calm

your nerves, but substances such as alcohol, Valium, or beta-blockers will only take you off your game. They may help you to feel less afraid, but they will impair your ability to give a good presentation. Here are some ways to help your body to relax naturally:

- **Release muscle tension.** Stretch your legs, and bend forward to stretch your back. Swing and shake your arms. Roll your shoulders and your neck. Lift your shoulders and then drop them. Clench your fists and release. All of these actions will help your muscles to relax. If your face feels tense, open your mouth wide, raise your eyebrows, squint, and clench your jaw to dissolve the tension in your facial muscles.

- **Breathe deeply.** If your breathing becomes shallow when you're nervous, you need to learn how to breathe from your diaphragm. You can learn how to do this by lying down and placing your hand on your abdomen. Feel your stomach rise on the inhale and lower on the exhale. Concentrate on this action until you can duplicate it while you're standing. When the fear takes hold, begin to slow your breathing and move it into your diaphragm. This is the fastest way to calm yourself in any high stress situation. The same process is used during medita-tion, and if you practise it, you will learn how to calm down quickly. It's a skill that you can utilize in numerous circumstances. As you breathe more deeply, you take in more oxygen and carbon dioxide, which signals your body that everything is OK. You can even try visualizing that your breath is moving into tense areas of your body. For example, if your knees are shaky, imagine breathing space into your knees until they relax. Try the same exercise with your neck and shoulders.

• **Look good.** The day of your speech, wear something that makes you feel good. Take special care with your grooming. The better you look, the better you will feel. Consider dressing a notch above the attendees as this will give you confidence.

• **Exercise.** You may find that exercising shortly before a presentation helps you to calm your nerves. Exercise also releases endorphins in your body, which help you to feel more positive.

• **Eat well.** Eating a balanced diet and taking vitamins will make it easier for you to stay calm. When you're healthy, you simply feel more relaxed. Vitamins B and C, calcium, and magnesium help to reduce stress, while some processed foods actually contribute to feelings of stress. Prior to your speech, be very careful about what you eat, and don't eat a large meal. Sugars may give you a quick pick-me-up, but they may also cause you to crash long before your speech is finished. Caffeine may keep you awake, but it could also intensify stage fright. Avoid foods that create phlegm, such as dairy products. Pay attention to how your digestive system responds to certain foods, and eat only those that will help to settle your stomach. Otherwise, you could increase those butterflies. The last thing you want is to experience indigestion or stomach growling during your presentation. Many times I am included in a meal before I deliver a presentation. I prefer not to eat immediately before speaking for two reasons. First, as suggested previously, it can play havoc with my energy level, and secondly, I do not want to cause a possible stain on my clothing or a piece of food in my teeth that I am unaware of. Both will completely distract me from delivering the best programme possible. I learned long ago to pretend to eat the meal placed before me. I cut up the food on my plate, move it around a bit, and do it again. I used to turn down the meal to prevent waste but unfortunately people would fuss over me, assuming I was on a restricted diet, or needed a special menu. In addition, when I did not have a meal in front of me it seemed like I was on stage and all eyes were on me. And I had not yet been invited to the platform!

During Your Speech

If you're one of those people who feel calm until the moment you step up to the podium, here are some tips to help you calm your nerves in the middle of your presentation.

- If your hands tend to shake, rest your notes on a podium. If there is no podium, use index cards, which will shake less noticeably than paper.
- Look for the friendliest faces in the audience, and make eye contact with them.
- If you try the old standby and imagine the audience in their underwear, you may end up feeling more uncomfortable in the long run. Instead, pretend that the audience is filled with people who love and admire you.
- Keep water nearby in case you get a case of dry mouth.
- Create notes that have your most important points in big, bold letters. This way, you need only glance at your index cards for cues.

No matter how frightened you may become about giving a speech, a toast, making an introduction, or asking a question or making a comment at a meeting, you can learn to manage your anxiety and actually enjoy the process. If you utilize all of the confident conversation skills you will learn in this book, from knowing your audience to timing to the creative use of silence, you will be armed with ways to combat your fears and project yourself as someone that your audience will both like and admire.

MASTER TECH TALK

Learn how to leave clear answering machine messages, send email messages and instant messages that won't be misinterpreted, and take advantage of online dating and networking tools.

In this age of fast electronic communications, it is much too easy to become casual and careless with messages that can be sent in a flash. But don't be fooled—messages that are sent via telephone or the internet are indeed *confident conversations*. In fact, your confident conversation skills are needed to an even greater degree in internet communications because without the benefit of voice inflection and facial expressions, misunderstandings are a frequent occurrence. And these miscommunications can lead to lost friendships, annoyed business associates, and awful conflicts at home and in the workplace.

Think of every type of communication as an opportunity to build a relationship. Every time you communicate with someone, whether in person, via telephone, email, or online chat, you are representing yourself, your company, your product, and/or your services. There is no advantage to carelessness in any of your exchanges.

Automation or Automaton?

Everyone has had the experience of calling a customer service department, only to find that it's nearly impossible to connect with a human being. You're asked to press numbers for information, but none of the options offered relate to your question. If you want to set your company apart from others in your industry, make sure your customers can get help when they need it—fast and efficiently. This means not only hiring telephone or online personnel, but giving them sufficient training to solve your customers' problems truly. In fact, your customer service representatives should be trained to handle many issues, rather than specialize in just one or two.

While it may appear to be expensive to hire and train human customer service personnel, doing so will develop extremely loyal customers. They will, in turn, tell others about the quality of your service. Statistics show that acquiring new business is about five times more expensive than keeping your current customers. Businesses with excellent customer service departments make more money in the long run because they maintain a solid customer base.

EMAIL ETIQUETTE

Achieving clarity in an email is more difficult than achieving it in letters written in longhand (assuming anyone writes such letters anymore). Snail mail letters take time to write, and allow for the luxury of thinking about what is said. Emails, on the other hand, are written so fast that you may hit the 'send' button before even bothering to proofread your message. As a result, emails tend to be riddled with typos, mistakes, and poorly constructed sentences that can easily be misunderstood. Below are some do's and don'ts to improve your email etiquette.

DOs

√ DO proofread your emails. Typos look careless and unprofessional, and your meaning can be lost in the process.

√ DO use all you have learned about clarity from previous chapters when writing your emails.

√ DO respond to emails if there will be any question about whether you received the message. Confirm meetings and appointments, and keep people informed about when they can expect to receive information from you.

✓ DO avoid sarcasm, and be careful with jokes, especially when they're directed at someone in particular. These can fall flat in online communications without the benefit of your facial expressions and vocal inflection. You may inadvertently offend someone, and your apology may not be enough to repair fully your relationships with the people involved.

✓ DO include an electronic signature to close your email. This becomes your trademark and lets everyone know who has sent the message. Include your title, the company name, and any important contact information. Keep your electronic signature short, however, without including too much information, such as a long sales pitch or quotes from famous people.

✓ DO pay attention to the subject line of your emails. If your email is in response to someone else's message and remains on point, allow the original subject line to continue. If you change topics, however, change your subject line accordingly. This will allow your recipients to organize their emails.

✓ DO keep your emails as short as possible. Consider that some people will read your messages on PDAs (personal digital assistants) and mobile phones. If your email is long, it may not be read at all.

√ DO create folders in your email program to organize and keep track of important messages.

DON'Ts

× DON'T leave out capital letters and punctuation, and don't use abbreviations such as BTW (by the way) or LOL (laughing out loud). These practices are simply unprofessional.

× DON'T use emoticons like smileys in business emails.

× DON'T use fancy colours or backgrounds in business emails.

× DON'T attach files to emails unless you know the files are welcome and free of viruses.

× DON'T forward political or comic emails to people unless you know they want to receive them.

× DON'T hit the 'Reply All' button when responding to an email unless you know everyone on the list and you're absolutely certain they all want to receive your message.

× DON'T say anything in an email that you wouldn't say in person.

× DON'T say anything in an email that you wouldn't want someone in your company to read. Internet communications are *not* confidential, despite firewalls and other security measures.

× DON'T carbon copy anyone who doesn't absolutely need to receive your email. Everyone's inboxes are cluttered enough!

× DON'T send bulk emails with everyone's addresses in the 'To' line even if it is for your thirtieth birthday party. In essence, you will be giving everyone's email addresses to each other, and this can set people up to receive spam. Type your own email address in the 'To' line, and put everyone else's email addresses under 'Bcc' (blind carbon copy).

× DON'T copy someone else's entire email before adding your comments. Copy and paste only the pertinent portion of the email, followed by your response. Make sure that your recipient can tell the original email quote from your response. You can add quotation marks to the original quote or change the font of your response to set them apart from one another.

× DON'T assume that someone will be able to answer your email immediately. I recently received an email from a colleague after twenty years of being out of touch. Less than twenty-four hours after she sent her original email, she sent another one saying she was disappointed that I obviously didn't care to speak to her. I had simply planned to respond to her a few hours later when I could sit down and write a comprehensive email. Sometimes, people are in meetings or conferences or travelling on long flights. A relative may even be in the hospital, or your email simply may not have reached its destination. Even if someone generally answers your emails quickly, don't make assumptions when a response isn't as fast as you expect. If *substantial* time passes without an answer, send another email or place a call to make sure your message was received.

× DON'T become upset by an email until you clarify the writer's intent. You may have misunderstood the message.

Build Virtual Rapport

Without realizing it, we miss rapport-building opportunities with colleagues and clients alike when we utilize email. If you are instigating the communication, begin with a nicety, just as you would in a voice interaction. 'Dear Jared, I hope you enjoyed your vacation.' Or 'Dear Ms. Burton, It has been a while since we have connected, hope all is well with you', or 'How have you been, Sarah? I'm hoping you can reply to me with the phone number for the window replacement company that ....' When responding to emails if the opportunity exists make a note in your reply about their email to you: 'Sounds like you have been working really hard', or 'Good to hear from you, too!'

INTERNET NETWORKING

Websites like LinkedIn.com, Facebook, and Myspace are helping people connect with one another for both business and personal reasons. Bloggers maintain profiles on LinkedIn, and as you ask people to join your network on the site, you connect with everyone in each of their networks, much like the branches of a tree. There is no end to the beneficial relationships that can result.

Online discussion groups and chat rooms are another way to build your network of contacts. Be sure to follow each group's guidelines, and treat your communications in discussion groups just as you would your emails and in-person comments. Maintain a professional if applicable and positive attitude at all times, never forgetting that your reputation is at stake.

THE NEW VIRTUAL MEETING PLACE

Finding a date through online personals is all about communication and delivery. The quicker the communication and delivery, the quicker you'll land a date. On some personals sites, for example, you can send a 'Wink', which is a quick, innocent way to flirt without sending a full-blown email. On others, you can send something known as an 'Icebreaker'. Another one gives you the option of putting a person you are interested in on a 'Hot List' to let him or her know that you're interested in talking. But even though these are effective ways to make the first contact, instant messaging (IM), which can be a great flirting tool, is a good way to initiate contact while you're online. Why? Because it allows you to be the person you always wanted to be 'in person'. For instance, maybe you've always been too shy to approach someone at school, at a party, or in a club.

All of those barriers are swept away when using IM; it is like an instant shot of courage. You can be confident, smooth and calm without reservations. And you can be spontaneous. After all, IM allows you to conduct real-time conversations, except you have time to think about what you'll say next—a huge benefit, which must be why it is so popular. Most of the major dating sites offer an IM system. But don't rush into it just yet.

Consider some ground rules that will ensure your IM experience is a successful one.

RULE #1: DO YOUR HOMEWORK BEFORE YOU INITIATE CONTACT

Your first IM to a new prospect should be engaging, interesting, and immediately engage the person you're interested in. To do that, you should know something specific about him or her. Make sure you've read their personal ad thoroughly before making contact; that way you might find something specific that you both have in common.

For instance, if the ad mentions that he or she is a graduate of Lancaster University, and you or someone you know is as well, that would be an excellent way to introduce yourself.

But even if you don't find anything in common, all is not lost. Read the personal ad and find something that interests you. Then ask a question about it. An example: 'Hello, I read your ad and you sound pretty interesting, especially when you talk about your career. Can I ask you a quick question?' If the reply is 'Yes' (and 99 times out of 100 it is), you have started a conversation. A very confident conversation. Ask a question that relates specifically to something you read in the personal ad. If you receive a reply, with a follow-up question, it's likely there is interest in engaging in more IM with you. You can also initiate contact using the following introductions:

1. A compliment: 'Hi, I just read your ad and I must say you have a great smile.' Leave it at that, and wait for a response.

2. Ask a question: 'Hi, I noticed you live in the West End. Have you ever been to Zaika?' Again, leave it at that, and wait for response.

3. Use the dating site system for credibility: '_____ sent me your ad as a potential match. What do you think? Are we a match?'

Once the IM thread gets started, this is where that continued dialogue will weave into a real conversation and ultimately a date.

RULE #2: DON'T BE A BLABBERMOUTH: BE CONVERSATIONAL, HUMOROUS, AND BRIEF

One of my challenges during travel occurs while I'm in a plane sitting next to somebody who won't shut up. It's the same with IM.

IM is really a face-to-face conversation, except you're doing it through a computer screen. However, if you're long-winded and boring, you will be dropped like a bad habit.

What to do: your sentences should be short, sweet and to the point—but with a flare that keeps interest. Keep it quick and conversational ... 'What have you been up to today?', 'How was your walk with the dog?', 'What went on at work today?'

The conversation can develop from there, and get deeper. But this will get things rolling.

RULE #3: BE CHARMING, BUT SUBTLE

Do not come at someone with a bunch of obvious pickup lines, or too cutesy remarks; be subtle. Always remember, IM is a means to an end. And the end is getting a date.

How to go from IM to a date depends largely on how quickly the dialogue between the two of you progresses. Expect it to take two IM sessions before the flirting gets more serious, like a telephone conversation. And of course, a few good telephone conversations typically convert into a real, live date. One more important thing: the personality you reflect during the IM session should also be reflected in the telephone conversation. Consistency and representing your true self is key to developing a lasting relationship.

Chatting with someone using IM on an online dating site is clearly one of the common rituals of courting today. Yet IM enhances other relationships as well. Watching as my husband Steve discovered the benefit of instant messaging was one of the great joys of my life. For years I encouraged, nagged and begged him to learn how to both read and send email. Steve is a very bright, interesting man who had an office manager to handle online communication at work and a wife to handle the same at home. That was until our son went to university thousands of miles away. A few weeks into this as Steve looked over my shoulder, I said: 'Jon is online.' Steve asked: 'How do you know?' and that began Steve's journey into the world of virtual conversation. He could not get enough. Although that was over four years ago, Steve proclaims to anyone that will listen, 'I have enjoyed some of the best conversations with my son with IM. I get more information about feelings and thoughts than I do during any of our phone conversations and even our face-to-face talks.' It is interesting that when a young man or woman has the opportunity to multi-task: watch TV, work on homework and IM and not be required to give eye contact, you get more 'communication' out of them. But it could be that humans are in fact well suited to the wireless age. 'Whenever there is a new technological advancement, people automatically want to think about how it could be bad for us,' says Kate Fox, a social anthropologist and director of the Social Issues Research Centre in Oxford. 'I take a different perspective: If this is so popular, what sort of deep-seated need is it fulfiling?' And I could not agree more with Kate Fox. Although texting is not my thing yet, I am beginning to get the hang of it, and have learned that it is a wonderful way to communicate with my children when they are unable (or unwilling) to answer their phones. Confident conversation is the ability to reach out and communicate in new and different venues with comfort and skill. Three years after Steve's initial dive into the internet he was challenged by the same child who was spending a term studying in Australia, many thousands of miles away. Turning Steve onto Skype was a whole lot easier!

ONLINE GROUPS

Follow the tips for email etiquette when participating in online groups, but below are some additional Do's and Don'ts for this type of specialized communication.

DOs

√ DO be watchful of your first posting to an online group. In fact, you might wait a few weeks until you know the group well before you post anything of substance.

√ DO read discussion group FAQs (frequently asked questions) and archives to get a sense of the group atmosphere and the people who post often.

√ DO vigilantly edit your postings to prevent typos and misunderstandings.

√ DO keep all of your messages concise and relevant to the discussion.

√ DO mention your knowledge, your purpose, products, or services when it's appropriate, but don't post a commercial about yourself or your company.

√ DO remain respectful of the ideas and opinions of others.

√ DO build relationships with individual members of an online discussion group, taking the time to cultivate these connections for your mutual benefit.

√ DO remember that any online discussion group has the potential of bringing you business, even if the topic is gardening or parenting. You never know the business contacts that can result from social connections.

√ DO ask participants of an online discussion group for assistance. People are usually more than willing to help. However, don't ask for huge favours. For example, asking for advice on places to visit in a particular city is fine, but asking to be recommended for a job by someone who has never met you is too much to ask. It would require them to put their own reputation on the line.

DON'Ts

× DON'T send a long personal introduction or biography to an online discussion group when you join. Make your introduction short and sweet to keep from being seen as overbearing.

× DON'T type messages in ALL CAPS. This is the equivalent of shouting online, and should only be used to emphasize something extremely important.

× DON'T use fancy formatting such as bold type, italics, or underlining. Some readers may have services that won't properly display this type of formatting. Keep your messages simple with plain text.

× DON'T jump into heated discussions until you are an accepted member of the group.

× DON'T be demanding or pushy. Establish your credibility gradually in online postings.

× DON'T take it personally if someone 'flames' you in a discussion group. Resist the temptation to post an angry message back. Resolve to be the better person, and stay on higher ground, keeping your reputation intact.

× DON'T just ask for favours—offer them in return and give readily whenever possible. You will eventually receive your generosity in return. However, never put your reputation at stake for someone else. Just as it's too much for you to ask to be recommended for a job by a member of an online group, learn to say no gently to anyone who asks for something that will put you at risk.

Be a Star on Conference Calls

It's always better to meet customers and colleagues in person, but in today's global marketplace, it isn't always possible. The next best thing is a dialogue using technology such as Skype or a conference call, and these may be audio or video. Below are some tips to ensure you make the best possible impression when dealing with conferences that are live, but not in person.

- Make sure you understand the technical aspects of the call. What happens if you press the mute button? If you press the hold button, will everyone hear music? If you put the call on speaker and rustle papers, will everyone be able to hear it?
- Ask everyone to identify themselves at the beginning of the call and each time they speak. It isn't always easy to distinguish voices on the telephone.
- Prepare for a conference call the same way you would prepare for an in-person meeting, and manage the time of the call in the same way.
- Turn off your mobile phones, and don't multi-task while on a conference call. Be certain that dogs barking, traffic, or noise outside your control is eliminated
- You may not be able to read body language during audio conference calls, but you can still listen for verbal cues from the participants that will help you tailor and adjust your responses.

Be a Star on Conference Calls

- Match your vocal tone and pace with the other parties', if possible, and you will more quickly develop a rapport.
- Thank everyone at the end of the call, and use the techniques discussed in Chapter 10 to end the conference on a positive note.

BUILD BETTER VOICEMAILS

Your outgoing voicemail message is often the first impression you make on a new friend or romance, colleague, or customer. This means you need to pay careful attention to how you sound and what you say. Always record your own outgoing message, and speak slowly, enunciating your words. Try to sound as friendly and upbeat as possible. If you have difficulty sounding cheerful, smile while you make your recording and think of something you enjoy or someone you love.

Establish who you are right away. You might say, 'Hello. You have reached the voicemail of Debra Fine, author of *The Fine Art of Confident Conversation*. Please leave a message at the tone or reach me via email at Debra@DebraFine.com.' You may opt to give your website address instead. Choose whichever address is shorter and easier to understand. If you need to offer a good bit of information in your message, give callers a way to bypass it and leave a message immediately.

When you leave messages for others, get to the point, mention the date and time of your call, and be clear about what you want. Bear in mind that the person you're calling may not remember you. Don't say: 'This is Debra Fine. Please call me back.' Instead, say, 'Hello, Steve. This is Debra Fine. It's 2 p.m. on 4 April. We met last night at the SOS Children's event and talked about getting together. I would like to set up a time that works for us both. Please return my call at 888-888-8888 between 9 a.m. and 5 p.m. or on my mobile phone in the evenings at 777-777-7777.' This will minimize the game of phone tag.

If you need information right away, say so in your message: 'Hello, Mr Smith. This is Ms Jones' secretary, Eileen, calling at 2 p.m. on Wednesday. I have put a hold on your reservations to Madrid next Tuesday, and will need your confirmation by no later than 4 p.m. on Friday. Please contact me at extension 234.'

Even if you know the recipient of your message has your telephone number, recite it in your message anyway. It's much easier for someone to jot it down than to hunt through their records for your contact information.

Whether your communication is on the telephone or the internet, all of your confident conversation skills apply. If you take electronic and telephonic messages as seriously as in-person meetings and interactions, you will create goodwill and positive 'buzz' that will follow you. Others will admire and want to emulate your confident attitude and pursuit of excellence.

THE OPEN ROAD AWAITS
(CONCLUSION)

Confident conversation covers a lot of ground. And as we discussed in the last chapter, the ways in which we communicate are constantly evolving. So, how can you best incorporate what you have learned? Approach it as you would a diet or learning how to sing. Digest the information, and then adapt and apply it to your own circumstances.

But don't forget that you also have to actually do it! As a master of many diets, I can tell you that purchasing the diet books and exercise videos is hardly enough. You have to make yourself use the information in a way that alters your life experience. Actively incorporate confident conversation skills into your life. Start slowly, and start small. Before I ran five kilometres for the first time, three city blocks was enough to make me gasp for air. Don't expect that you will be able to utilize all of the information right away. Give yourself time to try the techniques and see which ones work best for you. Consider it your own personal course, and grade yourself with compassion and patience. Approach the exploration with a sense of curiosity and discovery, and find a way to make it fun for you even when your nerves threaten to get the better of you.

It may be hard to ask for a date with the fear of rejection staring you in the face. But just like running, each time you ask for a date, you will build up your stamina. Keep track of how many 'no's' you receive until you hear a 'yes'. Track the positive and negative responses for a few months. Let's say you receive one 'yes' for every nine 'no's'. Guess what? Now, each time a prospective date says 'no', you can say thank you from the bottom of your heart because you're one more 'no' closer to your next 'yes!'

If you dread speaking in public, start with a toast for the assistant that is departing the firm. Practise in front of the mirror while taking deep breaths. Raise your hand in class and pose a question to the instructor, and try standing up when you ask the question. Volunteer at your child's school to present ten minutes of mathematics or art skills.

Never again approach a meeting without reviewing the chapter on managing a conversation, and in all your family and close relationships stop to look for danger signs that might point to potential conflicts based on divergent personalities or viewpoints. Write down the new skills you plan to incorporate during serious talks, taking mental note of what to watch for as you go along. Take the time to review your performance and set goals to improve the next time. Ask for feedback from a partner or friend, mentor or colleague regarding a specific technique you implemented.

Watch for any signs and signals of negative body language in yourself and others. Maybe your kids tease you that you flare your nostrils when you're angry. If so, you can count on the fact that you also do this at the office. The more aware you become of your body language, the more comfortable you will feel in your confident conversation skills. And as you develop your ability to notice non-verbal cues from others, have fun trying the different techniques to alter their reactions to you, learning what works and what doesn't.

Become the Robert De Niro of silence. Pretend that you're comfortable with gaps in the conversation, and you will begin to feel more at ease. Don't forget to stay silent, too, when confidentiality is necessary.

When insecurities get in the way, focus on others to take your mind off yourself. You'll project more positive energy in the process and develop your ability to be empathetic to others. And speaking of positive energy, don't forget to make your email messages as special and professional as your in-person communications.

Today's global landscape requires that we take the time to know our audiences. We need to learn how best to relate to other cultures, paying close attention to how our actions are viewed by those with dramatically different perspectives from our own. Even within our own culture, people can hold extremely divergent viewpoints that create unnecessary conflicts. You can't be expected to anticipate every possible scenario, but if you truly make the effort to cultivate confident conversation skills, you will have many techniques at your fingertips to handle different situations. These skills are all about improving the quality of your life, and they will offer you many ways to enhance your relationships. This translates to greater success in business, as well as happier exchanges in your personal life.

Most importantly, have confidence in your abilities. Practise positive *self-talk* to keep yourself motivated in your quest for better *confident conversation*. Just as you would regularly visit the scale to check the number of pounds that you've lost, keep track of your progress as you apply confident conversation techniques in your life and work. You will be able to see how your efforts are paying off, and the next thing you know, you'll be able to diagnose situations immediately, applying prescriptive remedies to turn your communications into truly valuable exchanges.

Confident conversation is something that you do not perfect overnight. Take every opportunity to practise the different interactions outlined in this book. Make the effort to evaluate your communication skills and the mistakes you make along the way. Learn from communicating confidently and you will continue to improve. As you get better and better, success will follow. Get talking confidently, and good luck!

THE FINE ART OF SMALL TALK

How to Start a Conversation in Any Situation
By Debra Fine

Do you hide in the bathroom or hang around the buffet table at social gatherings? Does the thought of striking up a conversation with a stranger make your stomach do flip-flops? Do you sit nervously through job interviews waiting for the other person to speak? Are you nervous when it comes to networking? Then it's time you mastered *The Fine Art of Small Talk*.

    With practical advice and conversation 'cheats sheets,' *The Fine Art of Small Talk* will help you learn to feel more comfortable in any type of social situation, from lunch with your boss to going to a party where you don't know anyone. *The Fine Art of Small Talk* teaches you how to:

- Start a conversation even when you think you have nothing to say
- Feel more at ease at parties, meetings and at job interviews
- Approach social functions with confidence
- Prevent awkward pauses and lengthy silences
- Steady your shaky knees and dry your sweaty palms
- Adopt listening skills that will make you a better conversationalist
- Turn every conversation into an opportunity for success

'Fine fully engages her audience. She involves readers in the discussion and gives lists of lines people can use'. *Library Journal*

ISBN 978 0 7499 2674 0